IVOR POWELL

MANNA FROM HEAVEN

Spiritual Food from the Word of God

kregel
PUBLICATIONS

Grand Rapids, MI 49501

Manna from Heaven: Spiritual Food from the
Word of God

Copyright © 1996 by Ivor Powell

Published by Kregel Publications, a division of Kregel, Inc., P.O. Box 2607, Grand Rapids, MI 49501. Kregel Publications provides trusted, biblical publications for Christian growth and service. Your comments and suggestions are valued.

Cover photograph: Patricia Sgrignoli, POSITIVE IMAGES
Cover design: Alan G. Hartman

Library of Congress Cataloging-in-Publication Data
Powell, Ivor, 1910–
    Manna from heaven: spiritual food from the Word of
God / Ivor Powell.
        p.   cm.
    Includes bibliographical references.
    1. Bible—Meditations. 2. Bible—Devotional use. I.
Title.
BS483.5.P69   1996   220.6—dc20   96-10319
                                                        CIP

ISBN 0-8254-3546-3

Printed in the United States of America
1 2 3 4 5 / 00 99 98 97 96

CONTENTS

PREFACE

Some years ago, I informed my friends that I had ceased writing books. I was wrong. I did not know at the time that infirmity would seriously curtail my evangelistic crusades, and that as a result, I would be compelled to spend more time in my study enjoying the privilege of research. Each day I came to my office hoping to find new treasures within the Word of God. I was like the children of Israel who went out each day to collect the manna sent from heaven. What I discovered was sweet, appetizing, and satisfying. A lifetime of study had already formed the habit of typing notes. Primarily, I did this to refresh my own soul and keep a record of my exploration into the lesser-known parts of the Bible. Slowly, but surely, my collection grew larger, and it became evident that another manuscript was appearing.

The studies enabled me to explore the less familiar parts of the Scriptures, and it became fascinating to discover "oil fields" in deserts, "gold" in the wilderness, and "precious stones" where I least expected to find them.

When writing the preface of an earlier book I compared the publication of a new volume to the launching of a ship. It is impossible to tell where the vessel may go before its usefulness terminates. Twenty-five years after *Bible Cameos* was published, a copy reached Southern India and was subsequently published in Telagu. The same thing happened in Tokyo where *Bible Windows* was translated into Japanese. Other books have been printed in French, German, and various languages. Now *Manna from Heaven* is about to begin its journey. May its cargo of "good news" refresh people in all parts of the world. It is my fervent desire that young ministers, and perhaps older ones, may reproduce these studies into sermons used by the Spirit of God.

I shall be indebted once again to Kregel Publications of Grand Rapids, Michigan, whose ability to transform a manuscript into a volume of great beauty constantly amazes me. I also acknowledge the skill with which my wife, Betty, edits all my materials. Her ability "to polish a diamond" is remarkable. Without her assistance my volumes may not have been completed. May the blessing of God make *Manna from Heaven* the most helpful of all my books.

IVOR POWELL

5

SECTION ONE
The Old Testament

*In the six hundredth year of Noah's life, in the second month,
the seventeenth day of the month, the same day were all the
fountains of the great deep broken up, and the windows of
heaven were opened. And the rain was upon the earth forty
days and forty nights (Gen. 7:11–12).*

It is interesting to know that heaven has windows, but unlike
those found on earth, they appear to be channels of communication.
The text is rendered "floodgates" in the marginal reading. Among
men, windows have two main purposes. They permit the entrance
of light and provide a way of looking at the immediate surroundings. Buildings without windows are vaults, useful only for storage.
Whether or not God's country possesses windows of the type known
upon earth may be debatable. God knew they would be necessary
among humans and instructed Noah to place a window into the first
ship ever constructed. This is generally believed to have been an
opening that extended all around the vessel just beneath the over-
hanging roof. Light was thus provided within the entire vessel and
ventilation made possible for every part of the ship. The Bible
explains that devastation came upon the earth when God opened
"the floodgates" of heaven.

Scholars now suggest that a change in the temperature of the
earth released enough water from the North and South poles to
cover the earth when "the fountains of the deep were unstopped."
Human intelligence cannot explain all the details of the ancient
catastrophe. Did God have widespread lakes in His country, and
were these released through the "floodgates"? Beyond this, everything is conjecture.

The Law Condemning . . . *How Serious*

There are five important Scriptures in which the windows of
heaven are mentioned. Ezekiel supplies other references that prove
windows were known during his generation. Each of the five
outstanding examples has its own significance, but when considered together they provide a progression of thought which, to
say the least, is informative. Throughout the ages the story of
Noah's ark has commanded attention and stimulated action. During the centuries liberal theologians dismissed the account as the

8

product of imaginative writers. Then data was forthcoming that refuted the critics. The archaeologists found clay tablets that endorsed the Bible story and as a result, expeditions went to Mount Ararat in Turkey to seek the remains of Noah's ark. These efforts were hindered by the authorities who refused to grant permission for exploration on the mountain. Remarkable reproductions of the clay tablets and relevant data can be found in the *Zondervan Encyclopedia of the Bible.*[1]

The Bible states the ancient catastrophe was a judgment on the immoral conduct of people who were filling the earth with corruption. God opened the windows of heaven to terminate their evil practices. Long afterward, Paul wrote: "Be not deceived; God is not mocked: for whatsoever a man soweth, that shall he also reap" (Gal. 6:7).

Many years ago I worked with a man who had recently retired from the Metropolitan Police Force in London, England. Frederick Dawes was a very fine Christian who belonged to a party of itinerant preachers. One night, I heard this brother describing how he was sent to guard a meeting in London where a nationally known atheist was to address a large gathering. My friend confessed he wanted to go into the building and drag the infidel from the platform. Yet, he had to prevent others from doing what he himself desired. During that meeting an usher rushed out to say the speaker had suffered a heart attack and died. The apostle Paul was correct when he wrote: "God is not mocked."

The Love Continuing . . . *How Sublime*

> Then said the LORD unto Moses, Behold I will rain bread from heaven for you; and the people shall go out and gather a certain rate every day, that I may prove them, whether they will walk in my law, or no (Exod. 16:4).

God's Ability

The account of how God rained down enormous supplies of manna in the wilderness is one of the most intriguing stories in the Bible. There were at least two million travelers who, so we are told, were fed twice a day. The Supplier provided four million meals every day for forty years! Allowing for the ten extra days used for what we call *leap years*, over the entire period the Lord provided 58 billion, 440 million meals. An average family of parents with two

9

children living today would need to live to be over 13 million years old before the supply could be exhausted. It seems ludicrous to play with figures such as these, but at least they demonstrate the amazing capability of God to minister to the need of His people. (See also "Eating Angels' Food" in this volume.)

God's Affection

More amazing than the continuing provision was the affection of God. The people whom He fed were rebellious and critical. It has often been claimed that "necessity is the mother of invention," and this was evident during World War II when food was in short supply in Britain. Small amounts became available at intervals, and the diet might have become intensely monotonous had not the women of the country devised ways to make a variety of appetizing meals. It seemed miraculous when they made apple pie without apples! The women of ancient Israel were equally inventive, for some of them baked the manna, and others made all kinds of desserts. God supplied the basic ingredient, but He was not a Heavenly Restaurateur supplying meals for lazy people. They had work to do, and when they did it they were satisfied; others who did not cooperate continued to complain. Yet the manna fell regularly, for the Lord never failed to honor His promise. The question may be asked: "What if He had ceased to care for His people?"

God's Abundance

It was never revealed how the heavenly food was made. Did the Almighty create or manufacture it? Speculation may lead to error, but it is safe to suggest that if God's angelic servants had any part in the production, the operators were always busy. Would it be wise to say that when the new generation of Hebrews entered the Promised Land, the angels enjoyed a well-deserved vacation? The ancient story proves the Lord can complete anything He commences.

The Lepers Convincing . . . *How Startling*

Then Elisha said, Hear ye the word of the LORD; Thus saith the LORD. Tomorrow about this time shall a measure of fine flour be sold for a shekel, and two measures of barley for a shekel, in the gate of Samaria. Then a lord on whose hand the

10

king leaned answered the man of God, and said, Behold, if the LORD would make windows in heaven, might this thing be? And he said, Behold, thou shalt see it with thine eyes, but shalt not eat thereof (2 Kings 7:1–2).

The inhabitants of the city of Samaria were in great distress; they were dying of starvation. The army of Benhaddad, the king of Syria, had surrounded the place, and apparently there was no escape.

And as the king of Israel was passing by upon the wall, there cried a woman unto him, saying, Help, my lord, O king . . . And the king said unto her, What aileth thee? And she answered, This woman said unto me, Give thy son that we may eat him to day, and we will eat my son tomorrow. So we boiled my son, and did eat him: and I said unto her on the next day, Give thy son, that we may eat him: and she hath hid her son (2 Kings 6:26–29).

Anxious parents were worried; their children were crying for food, and only the prophet Elisha remained calm as he sat with the elders of the city. Elsewhere the position was desperate. Benhaddad was a merciless enemy! Then suddenly the man of God predicted the famine was about to end, and within hours food would be plentiful. The prophet appeared to be absurd; his prediction was preposterous! When one of the noblemen heard this message, he sneered and said such a thing would only be possible if the Almighty opened windows in heaven. Probably he was very sarcastic, otherwise Elisha would not have pronounced his doom. "Thou shalt see it with thine eyes, but thou shalt not eat thereof."

Jehovah could have opened windows in heaven, but that was unnecessary. Instead he opened a door on earth. The invading armies of Syria had brought sufficient food for their army to continue the siege almost indefinitely. There was no need for supplies to be sent from heaven, when they were already close to the city.

Four lepers were in a terrible predicament. Leprosy had banished them from society, and surrender to the enemy meant certain death.

And there were four leprous men at the entering in of the gate: and they said one to another, Why sit we here until we die? If

11

we say, We will enter into the city, then the famine is in the city, and we shall die there: and if we sit still here, we die also. Now therefore come, and let us fall unto the host of the Syrians: if they save us alive, we shall live; and if they kill us, we shall but die. And they rose up in the twilight, to go unto the camp of the Syrians: and when they were come to the uttermost part of the camp of Syria, behold, there was no man there. For the Lord had made the host of the Syrians to hear a noise of chariots, and a noise of horses, even the noise of a great host: and they said one to another, Lo, the king of Israel hath hired against us the kings of the Hittites, and the kings of the Egyptians, to come upon us. Wherefore they arose and fled in the twilight, and left their tents, and their horses, and their asses, even the camp as it was, and fled for their life (2 Kings 7:3–7).

The lepers were mystified; they had come to seek mercy, but the enemy had disappeared! At first they thought it might be a trap, but when they explored the outermost part of the camp, they discovered the Syrians had made a hurried departure. The starving men ate some of the abandoned food, but then said, "We do not well: this day is a day of good tidings, and we hold our peace." When the citizens of Samaria heard the men's story, they were delighted until the unbelieving monarch suggested they might become victims of the wiles of the enemy. As the hope of the people began to wane, an unknown soldier courageously challenged the king's advice, declaring it would be folly to reject the message without first putting it to the test. He advised that volunteers be sought who would ascertain if the good news were true. When the young men went to the Syrian camp, they also found evidence that something had scared the enemy, and food was ready to be eaten. The Samaritans rushed to the gate of the city, and the sarcastic nobleman was trampled to death.

The Lord Commending . . . *How Stimulating*

It is generally accepted that Malachi ministered after the return of the exiles from captivity. His words were spoken to Hebrews who were confronted by immense problems. They had to earn a living and build homes for their families. Meanwhile, priests and other religious leaders were appealing for money to complete the temple and rebuild the walls of Jerusalem. People were reluctant to pay their tithe when personal debts remained. To present an offering to the Lord was reasonable, but to pay one tenth of their total income seemed an imposition. To such people God said:

> Bring ye all the tithes into the storehouse, that there may be meat in mine house, and prove me now herewith, saith the LORD of hosts, if I will not open you the windows of heaven, and pour you out a blessing, that there shall not be room enough to receive it (Mal. 3:10).

The laws regarding tithing were strict and exact; they referred to money, produce of the fields and many other things. The proceeds supported the priesthood and other religious activities. The Egyptians gave to Pharaoh two-tenths of their income (Gen. 47:24) but in Israel the tithe was only one-half of that amount. Probably it was easier for the Egyptians to meet the king's demand, for under the guidance of Joseph, even the peasants were prosperous. The tithe was mentioned early in history, for when Abraham met Melchizedek he gave tithes to him (Gen. 14:18–20). Throughout history tithing was considered to be an essential part of worship. It was not difficult to give money when the people were rich, but when food and money were scarce, obedience to God became a test of faith. Malachi urged Israel to obey the law, for that was the prelude of blessing. God promised to honor their sacrifice by opening the windows of heaven. He was saying: "Put me to the test, and you will discover I honor my word." Wise and loyal Christians know it is impossible to outgive the Lord. He is no man's debtor. Some people may be impoverished because they are stingy. The Savior said:

> Give, and it shall be given unto you; good measure, pressed down, and shaken together, and running over, shall men give into your bosom. For with the same measure that ye mete withal it shall be measured to you again (Luke 6:38).

---

1. *Zondervan Encyclopedia of the Bible,* vol. 2 (Grand Rapids: Zondervan Publishing House, 1976), 552.

NIMROD—WHOSE SUCCESS WENT TO
HIS HEAD AND DESTROYED HIS SOUL

*And Cush begat Nimrod: he began to be a mighty one in the
earth. He was a mighty hunter before the LORD: wherefore it
is said, Even as Nimrod the mighty hunter before the LORD
(Gen. 10:8–9).*

The name Nimrod comes from *maradh* which means *to rebel*,
and this might suggest it was acquired when the man rebelled
against society and God. Unless Cush, his parent, were a prophet, that unpleasant name would not have been given to a baby.
There was no way parents could foretell the future. It was impossible to predict the type of man their child would become.
Sometime during his adult career, Nimrod became a rebellious,
arrogant, dominating dictator who criticized Jehovah. His original name was abandoned, and what he became overshadowed
what he had been.

It has been estimated that more than one hundred years had
elapsed since the flood when Noah and his three sons commenced the task of replenishing the earth. However, since people lived to be very old in that era, that period would represent
only a short time in history. To recall what had happened a
century earlier would be the equivalent of a modern man remem-
bering what happened when he was a teenager. That may explain the rebellious attitude of Nimrod who founded the first
dynasty.

When Noah left the ark, he and his family entered an empty
world to make a new beginning. The Bible says that Noah begat
Ham; Ham begat Cush; Cush begat Nimrod. Therefore, Nimrod
was a great-grandson of Noah (see Gen. 10:6–8). It is probable
that in that age of longevity, young Nimrod could have listened
to his ancestor who built the ark. Already the inhabitants of earth
were increasing at an enormous rate. Each man desired to build
his own city, and the population, as commanded by God, began
to move further and further away from the ark's final resting
place. Eventually Nimrod was born, and it is interesting that
within the scope of a few sentences, the ancient writer emphasized that Nimrod was a mighty hunter. Animals had also increased and some of them had become a menace. Apparently no

other man gained fame through his exploits. It is possible that Nimrod protected and fed his neighbors and thus attracted attention. His dominance over animals eventually extended to men, who became the army that established the first dynasty. The Bible says: "And the beginning of his kingdom was Babel [Babylon], and Erech, and Accad, and Calneh, in the land of Shinar" (Gen. 10:10). Nimrod was the first man of renown to emerge after the flood, but he detested God. The Septuagint version of the Scriptures says: "Nimrod was a mighty hunter *against* the Lord," and this appears to be the key that unlocks the mystery of his life. Matthew Henry, the noted commentator, said:

> That which is observable and improvable in these verses is the account here given of Nimrod, v. 8–10. He is here represented as a great man in his day: he was resolved to tower above his neighbors. The same spirit that actuated the giants before the flood, now revived in him. There are some in whom ambition and affectation of dominion seem to be bred in the bone. Nothing on this side of hell will humble and break the proud spirits of some men.
>
> Nimrod was a great hunter; with this he began, and for this became famous to a proverb. Some think he did good with his hunting; he served his country by ridding it of the wild beasts which infested it. Others think that under pretense of hunting he gathered men under his command, in pursuit of another game he had to play, which was to make himself master of the country. Great conquerors are but great hunters. Alexander and Caesar would not make such a figure in Scripture history as they do in common history. Nimrod was a mighty hunter *against* the Lord, as translated in the LXX; that is, he set up idolatry. That he might set up a new government, he set up a new religion. *Babel was the mother of harlots.* He carried on his oppression and violence in defiance of God himself.[1]

Perhaps the oldest and most reliable explanation of Nimrod's power was given by Flavius Josephus, the famous Jewish historian. Concerning the present subject he wrote:

Now it was Nimrod who excited them to such an affront and contempt of God. He was the grandson of Ham, the son of Noah—a bold man, and of great strength of hand. He persuaded them not to ascribe it to God, as if it were through his means they were happy, but to believe that it was their own courage which procured that happiness. He also gradually changed the government into tyranny—seeing no other way of turning men from the fear of God, but to bring them into a constant dependence upon his power. He also said he would be revenged on God if he should have a mind to drown the world again; for that he would build a tower too high for the waters to reach, and that he would avenge himself on God for destroying their forefathers!

Now the multitudes were very ready to follow the determination of Nimrod, and to esteem it a piece of cowardice to submit to God; and they built a tower, neither sparing any pains, nor being in any degree negligent about the work; and, by reason of the multitude of hands employed, it grew very high sooner than anyone could expect; but the thickness of it was so great, and it was so strongly built, that thereby its great height seemed, upon the view, to be less than it really was. It was built of burnt brick, cemented together with mortar made of bitumen, that it might not be liable to admit water. When God saw that they acted so madly, he did not resolve to destroy them utterly, since they were not grown wiser by the destruction of the former sinners; but he caused a tumult among them, by producing in them divers languages, and causing that, through the multitude of those languages, they should not be able to understand one another. The place wherein they built the tower is now called *Babylon*; because of the confusion of that language which they readily understood before; for the Hebrews mean by the word *Babel*, confusion.[2]

Nimrod was a rebel determined to oppose the Almighty. The Lord commanded Noah to replenish the earth to allow his descendants to colonize the world. The arrogant hunter was unwilling to obey, and prior to the erection of his tower said: "Lest we be scattered abroad upon the face of the whole earth" (Gen.

11:4). Nimrod was a mighty hunter, a forceful leader, and a great builder. The reasons for erecting the tower might have been various. The city would offer a place of refuge, although it would have been unlikely that any man would challenge the existing leadership. The tower could have served as a lookout from which the surrounding country could be surveyed. As the ancient commentator suggested, it was meant to be so tall that if God ever decided to drown the world again, the waters would never submerge the structure. It has been suggested that since Nimrod was anti-God, he might have thought it possible to erect a tower sufficiently high to reach God's country, and thus make possible a direct attack on the armies of heaven. The idea might have been stupid, but since Lucifer also tried to dethrone Jehovah, it would be easy to believe that Nimrod, like the giants before the flood, had permitted Satan to control his life. This strange event became obnoxious to the Lord, who destroyed the project. The incident bequeathed to posterity truths that should never be forgotten.

The Guilty Conqueror ... *Constantly Criticizing*

As in retrospect the life of Nimrod is reviewed, certain facts stand forth in bold relief. Since he was aware of the experiences of Noah, his decision to remain in one locality was an indication he had no respect for the commandments of Jehovah. His plan to build a city led to disaster. Whatever his personal desire might have been, he was declaring war against God. That, to say the least, was extremely unwise. Any person who acted in this manner was committing suicide. Evidently he believed he could defy the Lord. Many years later Nebuchadnezzar, the king of Babylon, was equally foolish and was driven into the fields to eat grass as oxen (see Dan. 4:33). Unfortunately, when success goes to a man's head, he begins to think he can do anything. Perhaps Jesus had this fact in mind when He warned of the possibility of gaining the world at the expense of one's soul (see Mark 8:36).

The Great Calamity ... *Continuing Childless*

When God confused the language of the people and instituted conditions that ruined their building project, Nimrod probably became incensed, but his immediate reactions were never revealed. The building of the tower ceased, and confusion

17

paralyzed communications. During my work in Australia I stayed in the home of Walter Beasley, who at that time was intimately connected with archaeological activities in the Middle East. He described the clay tablets upon which was a sketch of a fish and three lines. He said this indicated an ancient customer's desire to buy three fish, but the buyer could not explain to the vendor what was desired. In a moment of time, God had disrupted all commercial activity, and the people had been confronted by circumstances beyond their control. What this meant to Nimrod is hard to imagine.

Every man desires to become a parent so that his children can continue using the family name. That the Bible writers valued genealogies endorses this fact. Men feared being impotent. All the details about Nimrod are surrounded by lists of men who begat children. Yet apparently Nimrod had no family. First Chronicles 1:10 states that "Cush begat Nimrod: He began to be mighty upon the earth." He *began* to be a mighty man! Does that suggest he never completed his task? He and his tower perished and disappeared from history. He had no heir. This unpleasant detail endorses the words of the psalmist, who wrote: "I have seen the wicked in great power, and spreading himself like a green bay tree. Yet he passed away, and, lo, he was not: yea, I sought him, but he could not be found" (Ps. 37:35–36). Men who leave God out of their lives have very little left.

A Glorious Contrast . . . *Christianity Confirmed*

Describing the tragedy of Babel, Moses wrote: "And the LORD came down to see the city and the tower, which the children of men builded. And the LORD said: Behold, the people is one, and they have all one language; and this they begin to do: and now nothing will be restrained from them, which they have imagined to do" (Gen. 11:5–6). Many years later, Luke, who was a Christian physician, described another event. "And when the day of Pentecost was fully come, they were all with one accord in one place. And suddenly there came a sound from heaven as of a rushing mighty wind, and it filled all the house where they were sitting. And there appeared unto them cloven tongues like as of fire, and it sat upon each of them. And they were all filled with the Holy Ghost, and began to speak with other tongues, as the Spirit gave them utterance" (Acts 2:1–4).

18

At Babel, sinners were trying to reach up to heaven; at Pentecost, God was reaching down to earth. In the former, God terminated the greatest building project ever planned. In the latter, the Holy Spirit descended to begin another building project—the church. This would not only reach to heaven but outward to embrace the world. Paul wrote: "[We] are built upon the foundation of the apostles and prophets, Jesus Christ himself being the chief corner stone; in whom all the building fitly framed together groweth unto a holy temple in the Lord" (Eph. 2:20–21). At the tower of Babel God confused the language to prevent listeners from understanding what was being said. At Pentecost He gave other tongues so that people would understand the word of God and thereafter repeat it around the world. After the tragedy of Babel people probably thought their world had ended. After Pentecost the citizens of Ephesus said: "These that have turned the world upside down are come hither also" (Acts 17:6). The men and women who survived the destruction of the tower of Babel went out to live and die; the men and women who followed Pentecost knew they would live eternally.

Poor Nimrod! He believed he could cope with every emergency of life, but he made a great mistake and died a lonely man. He lived for self and lived in vain. Only foolish people emulate the example of the ancient rebel.

1. *The Bethany Parallel Commentary on the Old Testament* (Minneapolis: Bethany House Publishers, 1985), 38.

2. *The Complete Works of Josephus,* trans. William Whiston (Grand Rapids: Kregel Publications, 1981), 30.

LOT—THE CAT ON A HOT TIN ROOF

And Lot sat in the gate of Sodom (Gen. 19:1).

And [God] delivered just Lot, vexed with the filthy conversation of the wicked: (for that righteous man dwelling among them, in seeing and hearing, vexed his righteous soul from day to day with their unlawful deeds) (2 Peter 2:7–8).

The title has always been a source of fascination, for it is difficult to understand why any cat would be content to remain on a hot tin roof when its paws seemed to be burning! Perhaps a mouse had made its home nearby, and in the hope of gaining a meal the cat was willing to endure pain. It is also difficult to comprehend why intelligent people remain in any place where life's greatest treasures are being destroyed. Perhaps they are willing to suffer in the hope of catching mice of another kind!

Poor Lot! He was a strange man, unable to escape from himself! Former experiences haunted him; he knew what needed to be done, but his feet would not cooperate with his heart. After the death of his father, the lad was an orphan with an uncertain future, but his uncle, Abraham, provided a home and a future for his nephew. The lad was not penniless, for he inherited whatever belonged to his deceased father. Under expert supervision, his flocks and herds increased enormously, and he was able to employ his own servants. The Bible reveals how the great increase in Lot's possessions led to strife regarding water rights. Eventually it became necessary for the two herds to be separated, and Abraham gave Lot permission to choose any direction in which to travel. The younger man saw the plains of Sodom were "like the garden of the Lord," and decided he would live in the lowlands. That decision proved to be the greatest mistake of his life. He was taken captive by warring kings, and but for Abraham's rescue, might have spent the rest of his life in captivity (see Gen. 14:1–16). Probably Lot was very excited when he took his herds to the plains of Sodom. He had become independent, could please himself; he was his own master. Unfortunately, he forgot to count the cost of his anticipated achievements.

20

Lot Compromised His Faith

It might be difficult to know what kind of faith he possessed. He had lived with Abraham, the friend of God, but there is no evidence that he ever loved the Lord. He never built an altar; he was too busy making money. Nevertheless, what he learned in childhood could not be easily forgotten. When Lot mingled with homosexuals and listened to their disgusting conversation, "he vexed his righteous soul." Their filthy topics were a terrible contrast to the inspired words of his uncle. It is thought-provoking that, whereas most nomads lived in their tents close to the herds, Lot became the owner of a house within the city.

The new citizen of Sodom knew that his life had been revolutionized. Earlier he sat and talked with a saint; now he was repelled by the company of abominable strangers. He remembered how Abraham knelt at God's altar to gain strength to overcome problems; the men of Sodom loved to reiterate their experiences when they exploited and manipulated each others' bodies. Apparently Lot desired to be important, and for that purpose abandoned his religious upbringing. He was able to sell his cattle in the cities of the plain and became a councillor, authorized "to sit in the gate" among the rulers of the city. He became the most miserable man in the area. He was truly like a cat on a hot tin roof, and the roof was getting hotter! Yet he did not leave, for he expected the mouse of his ambition to appear at any moment.

Lot Compromised His Fellowship

Lot received a great welcome from the inhabitants of Sodom; his cattle assured the Sodomites of a continuing supply of fresh meat. It was not long before he took a seat among the elders to give counsel to people who sought legal advice. When the other men amused each other with descriptions of lustful behavior, Lot remained silent. He was afraid to denounce them. They were potential customers. He should have walked away, but his legs seemed to be paralyzed. His hot tin roof was now almost unbearable, but the mouse was getting fatter!

At the close of an evangelistic service in New Zealand, a man said to me: "Sir, you have surely landed me in a hell of a mess." He continued: "I am one of three brothers; we are in business together. The government caught us once for not paying enough

21

income tax, but we outsmarted them by falsifying our books. But last night I came to hear you. After the meeting I went to the office where my partners were working late and asked them to buy me out, as I wanted to be clean! One brother locked the door, and then both of them beat me up. You surely landed me in a hell of a mess." It was evident he had discovered a disturbing truth. It is impossible to live in the smog of Sodom and still breathe the pure air of God's mountains.

Lot Compromised His Family

And Lot went out at the door unto them, and shut the door after him, and said, I pray you brethren, do not so wickedly. Behold now, I have two daughters which have not known man; let me, I pray you bring them out unto you, and do ye to them as is good in your eyes: only unto these men do nothing; for therefore came they under the shadow of my roof (Gen. 19:6–8).

And Lot went out, and spake unto his sons-in-law, who married his daughters, and said, Up, get you out of this place; for the Lord will destroy this city. But he seemed as one that mocked unto his sons-in-law (Gen. 19:14).

Why did this unhappy man give his daughters in marriage to two homosexual men? Why did he address the lustful mob as "*brethren*"? Was he so intent on retaining the favor of the citizens that he was willing to sacrifice his girls? When he said that his daughters had not known man, he revealed their marriages had never been consummated. The husbands were only interested in male companionship; the wives were only desired as house cleaners and cooks. Sodom was the classic example of the situation described by Paul.

Wherefore God also gave them up to uncleanness through the lusts of their own hearts, to dishonour their own bodies between themselves. Who changed the truth of God into a lie, and worshipped and served the creature more than the Creator, Who is blessed forever. Amen. For this cause God gave them up unto vile affections: for even their women did change the natural use into that which is against nature. And likewise also the men, leaving the natural use of the woman, burned in their lust one toward another; men with men working that which is unseemly, and receiving in themselves that recompense of their error which was meet (Rom. 1:24–27).

God ceased to strive with the sodomites, but Lot decided to live among them and welcomed two of their young men into his family. He sacrificed the happiness of his daughters to be more closely identified with potential customers. It is difficult to understand why this was done, but unfortunately the same kind of thing can be seen throughout the modern world. Men appear to be walking into quicksand. The more they proceed, the deeper they sink, and finally escape becomes impossible. Natives catch monkeys in Africa by placing an orange in a box or a tree. A small hole is left through which the animal can push its arm. When it grasps its prize and refuses to release it, it is impossible to pull the orange through the small aperture. To regain its freedom, the monkey must open its hand. The natives recognize this weakness and exploit it to trap the victim. Alas, people who once enjoyed freedom are now slaves because of their desire to hold and enjoy prohibited things.

Lot Compromised His Fortune

And it came to pass, when they [the angels] had brought them forth abroad, that he [the angel] said, Escape for thy life; look not behind thee, neither stay thou in all the plain; escape to the mountain, lest thou be consumed (Gen. 19:17).

The command given by the angels had been clear and precise; there was no time to lose; delay could be dangerous. Unfortunately, Lot's affections were still in Sodom. He was facing bankruptcy, and his outlook was appalling. Throughout the years he had worked unceasingly to increase his wealth, but now he was to be left with nothing. He had gambled and lost! Sodom was about to be destroyed by an earthquake and fire, and within a few hours the city would become ashes. Lot's cattle would disappear into gaping holes in the ground; his home and everything else would be destroyed by flames. He would be a homeless refugee with nothing to show for years of toil. Doubtless, Uncle Abraham would be willing to assist his impoverished nephew,

23

but financial help, or the replacement of herds, could never remove the ache from his soul, nor the shame from his mind. He believed himself to be a failure, and that increased his vexation. Did he know that he was delivered from Sodom through the faithful intercession of the old saint who lived in the mountains?

> And it came to pass, when God destroyed the cities of the plain, that God remembered Abraham, and sent Lot out of the midst of the overthrow, when he overthrew the cities in the which Lot dwelt (Gen. 19:29).

Did Lot ever reminisce and review the events which had transpired since he left Abraham's camp? Did he ever suffer remorse and wish he could relive his life? When the man was left with unpleasant memories, he became a classic example of the type of people mentioned by Paul. Lot was saved—"so as by fire." His life had been fruitless; he had nothing left of which to be proud. He could only enter into the eternal state with regret filling his soul. His mistakes should be a warning to every person acquainted with his story. The higher a man climbs, the more disastrous may be his fall.

Lot Compromised His Future

Abraham was a spiritual light that continued to burn brightly; Lot was a glimmer that quickly fizzled out in the darkness. He was so drunk that he lay on his bed utterly oblivious of his surroundings. He was unaware of the intention of his daughters, and would not have appreciated their scheme.

> And Lot went up out of Zoar, and dwelt in the mountain, and his two daughters with him; for he feared to dwell in Zoar: and he dwelt in a cave, he and his two daughters. And the firstborn said unto the younger, Our father is old, and there is not a man in the earth to come in unto us after the manner of all the earth: Come, let us make our father drink wine, and we will lie with him, that we may preserve the seed of our father (Gen. 19:30–32).

We were first introduced to Lot when he was adopted by Abraham. He became a regular member of the patriarch's family and was present when his benefactor knelt at the family altar. Now we see him lying in a drunken stupor, making possible the birth of the Moabites and Ammonites who became the deadly enemies of the Hebrews (see Gen. 19:37–38). Lot was a man who loved to travel downhill where progress was easy but costly. If a man were commissioned to write a list of the great men of the Bible, the writer would not include Lot. That name would be out of place among others such as Abraham, Isaac, Jacob, Joseph, Moses, the prophets, and the apostles of the New Testament. Yet, the fact remains that Lot could have been included with distinction with those whose names are immortal. The writer to the Hebrews made such a list and said of Abraham: "By faith . . . he looked for a city which hath foundations, whose builder and maker is God" (see Heb. 11:9–10). Lot looked for a city that had business possibilities. Alas, it was a place built on unreliable foundations—it was called Sodom, a center of infamy and lust. No true believer could find peace in such surrounding. The future of this disappointing man went up in flames!

HAGAR—WHO FOUND A WELL IN
THE WILDERNESS

And Abraham rose up early in the morning, and took bread,
and a bottle of water, and gave it unto Hagar, putting it on
her shoulder, and the child, and sent her away: and she
departed, and wandered in the wilderness of Beer-sheba. And
the water was spent in the bottle, and she cast the child under
one of the shrubs. . . . And God opened her eyes, and she saw
a well of water; and she went, and filled the bottle with water,
and gave the lad drink (Gen. 21:14–15, 19).

The story of Hagar the Egyptian maid who was given by
Sarah to Abraham is one of the most pathetic in the Scriptures.
When Abraham and his wife were called by God to leave Ur of
the Chaldees and proceed to Canaan, they were promised their
seed would inherit the land to which they journeyed. After ten
years of fruitless waiting for their first child, the would-be parents
believed their prayers would never be answered. Sarah then
decided to give her servant to Abraham so that the maid could
bare a child.

Now Sarai Abram's wife bare him no children: and she had
an handmaid, an Egyptian, whose name was Hagar. And Sarai
said unto Abram, Behold now, the LORD hath restrained me
from bearing: I pray thee, go in unto my maid; it may be that
I may obtain children by her. . . . And Sarai Abram's wife
took Hagar her maid the Egyptian, after Abram had dwelt ten
years in the land of Canaan, and gave her to her husband
Abram to be his wife (Gen. 16:1–3).

Clay tablets discovered by archaeologists in that part of the
world have revealed this practice was common during Sarai's
lifetime. It provided barren women with a chance to become
foster mothers; furthermore, the real mother could not be expelled from the family. When Abram yielded to his wife's per-
suasion, it was evident that he believed she was too old to become
a mother. Unfortunately, his conduct caused serious repercussions and resulted in the tension which now exists between Jews
and Arabs. It is reported that after Hagar conceived her child,

she despised her mistress and ruined the tranquillity of the family. Many years later, Solomon said that a handmaid who became heir to her mistress could become a source of annoyance (see Prov. 30:23). A spiteful, nagging woman is a pest, and Sarai, seeing scorn in the eyes of Hagar, began to detest her servant. Probably the maid suffered because of the treatment of Sarai, and finally ran away. An angel of the Lord discovered her close to a well in the wilderness and instructed her to return to Abram's camp where she remained for several years after her son was born. Coming events were casting their shadows before. Alas, the lad grew to be like his mother, and that led to trouble.

And Sarah saw the son of Hagar the Egyptian, which she had born unto Abraham, mocking. Wherefore she said unto Abraham, Cast out this bondwoman and her son: for the son of this bondwoman shall not be heir with my son, even with Isaac. And the thing was very grievous in Abraham's sight because of his son (Gen. 21:9–11).

Perhaps Abraham would have refused to do as his wife suggested had not the Lord solved the family problem. God instructed him to do as his wife desired. He therefore gave food and drink to Hagar and sent her into the wilderness. That was a difficult decision, for Abraham loved Ishmael. As was to be expected, the supply of water soon disappeared, and as despair and thirst overwhelmed the distraught mother, she placed her son in the shade of a bush and wept. Her tumultuous world apparently was about to end in disaster, and she could not prevent the catastrophe. Life teaches that when people reach the end of their resources, God is never far away.

And God opened her eyes, and she saw a well of water; and she went and filled the bottle with water and gave the lad drink (Gen. 21:19).

God's well was infinitely better than Abraham's bottle, and that lesson has been demonstrated throughout history. Amid all the tangled skeins of Hagar's life, God was weaving a glittering pattern of kindness that overshadowed everything else. He understood her problems, and, although she did not know it at the time, God was making all things work together for her good. Ultimately that woman must have known Jehovah was more to be desired than all the glittering idols seen in Egypt.

Hagar's New Family . . . *Undesired*

> Now Sarai, Abram's wife, bore him no children: and she had an handmaid, an Egyptian, whose name was Hagar (Gen. 16:1).

Somewhere in Egypt lived a young woman who was destined to become the wife of Abraham. Information regarding the circumstances that led to this event is limited. She might have been sold by impoverished parents, or she could have been given by Pharaoh, the ruler of Egypt, to his illustrious visitor from Ur of the Chaldees (see Gen. 12:17). Whatever the reasons may have been, the young woman was suddenly confronted by the loss of her family and friends and was compelled to accompany strangers into the unknown. It was never revealed whether this pleased or distressed the girl, but in a realm where women had no authority, she accepted the inevitable and became the personal attendant of Abraham's wife. She worked around the encampment, but her life was without luster until one day she was summoned to appear before her mistress. She was informed a marriage was being arranged; she was to become Abram's new wife in order to bear a child for the barren Sarai. This was customary, but whether or not Hagar was pleased is debatable.

The new relationship with Abraham gained for her a new respect within the family, and she undoubtedly appreciated the increasing interest shown by her master. Her future became bright with prospect and hope, and the pregnancy pleased Sarai. Everybody appeared to be excited, and the Egyptian became a center of attraction within the camp. Each person seemed anxious to help, and she assumed new importance within the family. Unfortunately, the inflation of her ego became a threat, and her attitude was the forerunner of disaster.

Hagar's New Feud . . . *Unappreciated*

> And when [Hagar] saw that she had conceived, her mistress was despised in her eyes. . . . And when Sarai dealt hardly with her, [Hagar] fled from her face (Gen. 16:4, 6).

And Sarah saw the son of Hagar the Egyptian, which she had born unto Abraham, mocking. Wherefore she said unto Abraham, Cast out this bondwoman and her son, for the son of this bondwoman shall not be heir with my son, even with Isaac (Gen. 21:9–10).

Hagar's sun had been eclipsed; darkness was spreading through her world. The displeasure that commenced with her pregnancy increased enormously after the birth of Ishmael. Her sudden, but temporary, flight from Sarah had been interrupted by the angel of the Lord, but years later this was followed by total banishment from the camp. The infuriated Sarah demanded her expulsion, and Abraham yielded to the demand. When Hagar and her teenage son were homeless and hopeless, she placed her weary boy in the shade of a bush and went away to weep and wait for death. There is no fury that can equal that of a woman scorned! Perhaps it is safe to assume that Hagar was responsible for her distress, but there may have been another reason for Sarah's antagonism. Laws regarding a family inheritance were explicit. The firstborn son received twice as much as any other son. This was known as the *birthright*. Ishmael was the first son of Abraham and consequently after the father's death would have received more than Isaac and would have been the leader of the family. Sarah could not tolerate that possibility. Apparently, neither woman had much faith in the providence of the Almighty. Hagar could not believe her life was still of interest to the Lord, and Sarah could not believe Jehovah could control His own affairs without her interference. "Now faith is the substance of things hoped for, the evidence of things not seen" (Heb. 11:1).

Hagar's New Freedom . . . *Unparalleled*

Self-pity had made Hagar blind to several facts. She failed to see the well in the wilderness because she could not see beyond her personal need. People who stare at the earth seldom see stars, and those submerged in an ocean of grief sometimes fail to see a hand outstretched to help. Maybe the well was hidden by bushes, for that was, and still is, customary in the desert. When the angel of God called to her, he said: "What aileth thee, Hagar?" He knew her by name! Had she been a Hebrew, the daughter of a priest or even the wife of a prophet, God's action would have been understandable, but she was an outsider—a pagan, an Egyptian. Perhaps that was one of the earliest revelations—that God was capable of loving the whole world. When that forlorn mother filled her bottle with water and went to alleviate her son's thirst, a new world opened before her. God did not recognize racial barriers; he saw her plight and supplied what was needed. The ancient account tells that God heard the voice of the lad. Had the Almighty desired their death, He would not have helped them. Suddenly the woman began to know that in spite of circumstances, there was hope for them in that inhospitable wilderness. The darkest night may be followed by a glorious dawn. Malachi was correct when he wrote: "But unto you that fear my name shall the Sun of righteousness arise with healing in his wings; and ye shall go forth, and grow up as calves of the stall" (Mal. 4:2). For the first time in her life Hagar was a free woman, and as the Gospel says: "If the Son therefore shall make you free, ye shall be free indeed" (John 8:36).

Hagar's New Future . . . *Unprecedented*

And God was with the lad; and he grew, and dwelt in the wilderness, and became an archer. And he dwelt in the wilderness of Paran: and his mother took him a wife out of the land of Egypt (Gen. 21:20–21).

The word "*well*" has also been translated "fountain and spring." It was close to this supply that life began anew for Hagar and her son. Water in a desert is a rare commodity, and it may be assumed many animals went there to drink. Possibly that was the chief reason why Ishmael became an archer. The boy's skill with his bow and arrows guaranteed there would always be a plentiful supply of meat. Somewhere near to this oasis they built their first home; it might have resembled a Bedouin tent made of animal skins, or it could have been made of mud bricks baked in the sun. Time passed and the lad became an adult.

Normally, most marriages were arranged by fathers, but Hagar accepted this responsibility of finding a wife for Ishmael. Probably she and her son discussed this project when they talked together in the evenings. They could not return to Abraham's camp, and since her native country was close at hand, it was decided to seek a bride in Egypt. Through trading skins, they

30

had ceased to be poor, and were able to purchase a slave. If Ishmael accompanied his mother into Egypt, he might have won the affections of a young lady. It would be interesting to know the answers to questions that might be asked. The Scriptures simply say: "His mother took him a wife out of the land of Egypt" (Gen. 21:21). Later, in the seclusion of their primitive home, Ishmael's wife gave birth to their first child whom they named Nebajoth, which meant *High Place.*

Whether or not there was special significance in that name is uncertain. Perhaps Hagar regarded the birth of her first grandchild as the greatest experience of her life, the highest plateau of happiness she could ever reach. Their proximity to Egyptian villages made trading profitable, and Ishmael had no difficulty in supporting his family. The kindness of Jehovah was apparent. His promise to make Ishmael a great nation was beginning to be fulfilled. Hagar had progressed magnificently since her expulsion from the employment of her former mistress. She was beginning to believe that even dark clouds had silver linings.

Hagar's New Fame . . . *Unique*

And these are the names of the sons of Ishmael, by their names, according to their generations: The first born of Ishmael, Nebajoth; and Kedar, and Adbeel, and Mibsam, and Mishma, and Dumah, and Massa, Hadar, and Tema, and Jetur, and Naphish, and Kedemah: These are the sons of Ishmael, and these are their names, by their towns, and by their castles; twelve princes according to their nations. And these are the years of the life of Ishmael, an hundred and thirty and seven years: and he gave up the ghost and died; and was gathered unto his people (Gen. 25:13–17).

When the twelve sons of Ishmael grew to manhood, they married and had their own families, and the influence of the Ishmaelites spread throughout the wilderness areas. The men formed an alliance which struck terror into the hearts of enemies. They turned unproductive areas into farmlands, and every high place became heavily fortified. Their *castles* were impregnable. Throughout the entire area Hagar was regarded as a queen. The aging grandmother was adored by her children, and respected by her descendants. Nothing is known of her death, but when reviewing her life, she could have expressed similar sentiments to those uttered by Paul: "And we know that all things work together for good to them that love God, to them who are called according to his purpose" (Rom. 8:28). It is almost beyond comprehension that a girl who had been ejected from the camp of Abraham should have reached unimaginable heights of eminence. God had truly blessed Ishmael, and the proud grandmother rejoiced when she saw the promises of God were being fulfilled!

*Then said the LORD unto Moses, Behold, I will rain bread
from heaven for you; and the people shall go out and gather a
certain rate every day (Exod. 16:4).*

*And the children of Israel did eat manna forty years . . . until
they came unto the borders of the land of Canaan (Exod. 16:35).*

*Yea, they spake against God; they said, Can God furnish a
table in the wilderness?. . . And [God] had rained down
manna upon them to eat, and had given them of the corn of
heaven. Man did eat angels' food (Ps. 78:19, 24–25).*

*The people asked, and he brought quails, and satisfied them
with the bread of heaven (Ps. 105:40).*

The account of how God sustained the children of Israel during their journey from Egypt to Canaan has always commanded
attention. Prophets referred to it, the psalmist wrote about it, the
Savior used it as an illustration, the apostles preached about it,
and today foolish critics argue about it. There are three postures
taken by people who speak about this incident in the wilderness.

1. Denial

Unbelievers state the story is based on fantasy: it never happened. They say the same about all the supernatural miracles
mentioned in the Bible. Unless they can explain things according to natural laws, the incidents are dismissed as untrue.

2. Dilution

Some people believe the miracle was unnecessary, for the people
gathered a substance produced by the *tamarix manifera* trees that
grow profusely in that part of the world. For example, Werner
Keller, the German journalist who explored the Middle East, wrote
a book entitled *The Bible as History* and discussed the manna that
fell in the wilderness. He says: "In every valley throughout the
whole region of Mt. Sinai, there can still be found 'The Bread of
Heaven,' which the monks and Arabs gather to preserve and sell to
strangers who pass that way." These words were written in 1483 by

Breitenbach, Dean of Mainz, in an account of his pilgrimage to Sinai. "The same bread," he continues, "falls about daybreak like dew or frost and hangs in beads on grass, stones and twigs. It is sweet like honey, and sticks to the teeth. We bought a lot of it." Keller then lists a number of expeditions whose findings were supportive of this description. One of the explorers named Bodenheimer said: "The taste of these crystallized grains of manna is peculiarly sweet. It is most of all like honey when it has been left a long time to solidify." "It was like coriander seed, white; and the taste of it was like wafers made with honey" (see Exod. 16:31). The tamarix tree that produces this manna can still be found in that part of the Middle East. The Bedouins knead the globules into a puree which they consume as a welcome and nourishing addition to their often monotonous diet. The tamarix trees grow in profusion in Sinai and along the Wadi of Arabah right up to the Dead Sea.[1]

3. Defense

This German author was a sincere Christian who wished to vindicate the accuracy of the Scriptures. His opinion, however, may not represent the truth expressed in the Bible. Arthur W. Pink, the noted author and expositor, also researched this subject, and his comments are interesting. He wrote: "It is striking to note how the supernatural is evidenced in connection with the giving of the manna. In Exodus 16:16 we read, 'This is the thing which the LORD hath commanded, gather of it every man according to his eating, *an omer for every man*, according to the number of your persons; take ye every man for them which are in his tents.' Now, a conservative estimate of the total number of Israelites who came out of Egypt would be two million, for they had more than six hundred thousand men able to go forth to war (see Num. 1:45–46). An 'omer' was to be gathered for every one of these two million souls, and an omer is the equivalent of six pints. There would be twelve million pints, or nine million pounds gathered daily, which was four thousand five hundred tons. Hence, ten trains, each having thirty cars, and each car having in it fifteen tons, would be needed for a *single* day's supply. Over a *million tons* of manna were gathered annually by Israel. And let it be remembered this continued for forty years! Equally wonderful, equally miraculous, equally Divine is the Bible."[2] This viewpoint is correct, for without divine assistance the nation

34

would have perished in that inhospitable region. If God intended to bring the Hebrews into the land of Canaan, it was incumbent upon Him to sustain them until that became possible.

The Manna Was Divinely Provided . . . *Perfectly Amazing*

Then said the LORD unto Moses, Behold, I will rain bread from heaven for you (Exod. 16:4).

And the whole congregation of the children of Israel murmured against Moses and Aaron in the wilderness: And the children of Israel said unto them, Would to God we had died by the hand of the LORD in the land of Egypt where we sat by the flesh pots, and where we did eat bread to the full; for ye have brought us forth into this wilderness to kill the whole assembly with hunger (Exod. 16:2–3).

Moses and Aaron must have been very frustrated. The stay at Elim, where twelve wells of water had quenched the thirst of the people, had been followed by increasing problems. The wells could not continue to meet the demands of such a large multitude, and the limited shade offered by seventy palm trees could not shield everybody from the relentless heat of the sun. Everybody was complaining and the camp was in an uproar. Animals were listless, children were crying, and parents were becoming increasingly resentful. Then came the voice of God to reassure Moses. The Lord said, "Behold, I will rain bread from heaven for you." What followed almost beggared description.

Throughout the night, the bread fell like a gigantic snowstorm until the strange substance covered the entire camp. When the sun arose, its light shone upon a scene of resplendent beauty. The first men to see the spectacle wondered if they were dreaming, for such a spectacle had never been seen. Suspiciously, they tasted "the bread of heaven," which seemed like wafers made with honey. The fact that enormous quantities had fallen from the sky was temporarily forgotten, as the excited Israelites enjoyed an early morning picnic. Somewhere in the crowd Moses stood and whispered: "Thank you, Lord."

They said therefore unto him, What sign shewest thou then, that we may see, and believe thee? what dost thou work? Our

35

fathers did eat manna in the desert; as it is written, He gave them bread from heaven to eat. Then Jesus said unto them, Verily, verily, I say unto you, Moses gave you not that bread from heaven; but my Father giveth you the true bread from heaven. For the bread of God is he which cometh down from heaven, and giveth life unto the world. Then said they unto him, Lord, evermore give us this bread. And Jesus said unto them, I am the bread of life: he that cometh to me shall never hunger; and he that believeth on me shall never thirst (John 6:30–35).

A crowd of people stared at the Savior. They had witnessed an astonishing miracle, but doubt was paralyzing their faith. "They said therefore unto him, What sign shewest thou then, that we may see, and believe thee? What dost thou work?" (John 6:30). It was evident that God alone could supply the Bread of Life— no other source was available. When Jesus claimed to be *The True Bread*, He implied the manna was a foreshadowing of a greater event still to come.

Deliberately Possessed . . . *Personally Accepted*

This is the thing which the LORD hath commanded, Gather of it every man, according to his eating, an omer for every man, according to the number of your persons; take ye every man for them which are in his tents (Exod. 16:16).

The nights in the wilderness were extremely exciting. As the darkness approached, even the children waited for their first glimpse of the falling manna. It descended with the grace of snowflakes. Perhaps the people were afraid to go outside their tents, but when the dawn came it seemed as if angels had covered the ground with a huge white blanket. As the manna reflected the magnificence of the rising sun, the people beheld a scene of loveliness never before witnessed. Nevertheless, the fact remained that families could have starved to death. The manna was useless unless it was gathered. Moses was very explicit when he instructed the heads of households to collect what was necessary for their families. It would appear to be inconceivable that men would neglect or refuse to do what was urgently essential. The same truth applied to the gathering of the quail that

36

were brought by strong winds to the area. If people refused to obey the instructions given, death was inevitable. The Hebrews chose between sustenance and starvation. If they obeyed God, they lived; otherwise, they perished.

Many years later the Savior expounded that Scripture and emphasized that the manna in the wilderness did not supply eternal life; the people who ate it eventually died. He alone was the true Bread of Life, able to supply immortality.

> Verily, verily, I say unto you, He that believeth on me hath everlasting life. I am that bread of life. Your fathers did eat manna in the wilderness, and are dead. This is the bread which cometh down from heaven, that a man may eat thereof, and not die. I am the living bread which came down from heaven: if any man eat of this bread, he shall live forever: and the bread that I will give is my flesh, which I will give for the life of the world (John 6:47–51).

It is interesting that, although the heads of households were commanded to gather manna for their dependents, each individual was required to partake for himself; the father could only gather food for his family—they had to eat it! The Lord said: "Him that *cometh* to me I will in no wise cast out" (John 6:37).

Delightfully Pleasing ... *Possibly Angelic*

> Though he had commanded the clouds from above, and opened the doors of heaven and had rained down manna upon them to eat, and had given them of the corn of heaven. Man did eat angels' food (Ps. 78:23–25).

> And the manna was as coriander seed, and the colour thereof as the colour of bdellium. And the people went about, and gathered it, and ground it in mills, or beat it in a mortar, and baked it in pans, and made cakes of it: and the taste of it was as the taste of fresh oil (Num. 11:7–8).

Abber, the Hebrew word which has been translated *angels*, means strong or mighty and is used regarding princes (Ps. 68:31) and nobles (Job 24:22). It could be rendered "food of nobles and princes," that is, food of richer quality than is found on the tables of peasants. The immediate context would seem to require the translation used in the Authorized Version, for the food is said to have come down from heaven. It is rendered "food of angels" in the Septuagint, the Vulgate, other ancient versions of the Bible, and by Luther."[3]

The psalmist was convinced the manna was food upon which heavenly beings feasted. If that viewpoint was correct, then angels had been thrilled, sustained, and nourished by their fellowship with the Son of God. The text might therefore provide an insight into the diet of angelic beings.

It is worthy of consideration that the manna was taken by the Hebrew women and ground in mills, beaten in mortars, baked in pans, and made into cakes and other delicacies. Their efforts were phenomenal, for what they produced resembled the taste of fresh oil. All Christians should consider this fact. God sent the Bread of Life, but much depends upon how it is appropriated. The Savior is able to help His followers in every circumstance of life. People who never "explore" fellowship with Christ may say as did the mixed multitude in Israel: "But now our soul is dried away" (Num. 11:6).

Many years ago, I heard an old man giving a testimony. He said: "Brothers and Sisters, I love Sunday when I can come to church and get my batteries charged by listening attentively to the sermons. Then on Monday and Tuesday I feed on them, but by Wednesday I have forgotten what I heard. During Thursday, Friday, and Saturday, I wait for Sunday so I can recharge my batteries." I wondered what might have happened if the preacher had an off day! God gave us oxygen to breathe *every moment of every day*. He also supplies "angels' food" to produce similar results.

Definitely Prolonged . . . *Purpose Accomplished*

And the children of Israel did eat manna forty years, until they came to a land inhabited; they did eat manna, until they came unto the borders of the land of Canaan (Exod. 16:35).

Evidently, God was able to complete what He commenced. The continuance of His blessing did not depend upon the worthiness of Israel, but upon His own faithfulness. There were many occasions when the Hebrews displeased the Lord, when their desire to return to Egypt was offensive. Yet, in spite of their complaints, the manna continued to descend.

> And the mixt multitude that was among them fell lusting: and the children of Israel also wept again, and said, Who shall give us flesh to eat? We remember the fish, which we did eat in Egypt freely; the cucumbers, and the melons, and the leeks, and the onions, and the garlick. But now our soul is dried away: there is nothing at all, beside this manna, before our eyes (Num. 11:4–6).

We should not quickly condemn the children of Israel, for unfortunately, we resemble them; we are selfish and like to control our destiny. When prayers are not answered favorably, we are displeased and begin to question God's wisdom. The "food of Egypt" was associated with bondage. The patience of God is almost beyond comprehension. Throughout the forty years in which Israel wandered in the wilderness, the Lord's mercy never diminished. The manna continued to fall until the land of milk and honey was just across the river. Thomas O. Chisholm might have been reviewing Israel's journey when he wrote:

> Great is Thy faithfulness, O God my Father,
> There is no shadow of turning with Thee;
> Thou changest not, Thy compassions, they fail not;
> As Thou hast been, Thou forever wilt be.
> Great is Thy faithfulness!
> Great is Thy faithfulness!
> Morning by morning, new mercies I see;
> All I have needed Thy hand hath provided—
> Great is Thy faithfulness, Lord unto me!

1. Werner Keller, *The Bible as History* (New York: William Morrow and Company, 1956), 117–120.

2. Arthur W. Pink, *Gleanings in Exodus* (Chicago: Moody Press, 1979), 124–25.

3. Albert Barnes, *Barnes' Notes on the Psalms,* vol. 2 (Grand Rapids: Baker Book House, 1978), 298.

My home in Wales was surrounded by mountains which presented an escape from the busy life of the valley. The constant traffic on the narrow streets, the shops, the people seemed to be restrictive, so I developed the habit of climbing the hills where the silence was unbroken. I had a friend called Clifford, and together we shared fellowship. He became a missionary, and I, an evangelist, but in those days we preached to each other. He practiced on me, and I on him, and maybe even the angels laughed. It was to be expected that mountains would always attract me. I have worshiped on Mount Calvary, climbed Dr. Boreham's Mount Hobart in Tasmania, stood on Mount Carmel in Israel, Table Mountain in Capetown, South Africa, and looked with awe on the mighty Himalayas in northern India. The Lord appreciates my interest in mountains, for He designed every one of those lofty places.

Climbing Mount Sinai with Moses . . .
The Place of Revelation

> And the LORD came down upon mount Sinai, on the top of the mount; and the LORD called Moses up to the top of the mount; and Moses went up (Exod. 19:20).

Moses was climbing into the holy mountain, but progress was slow. The entire area was shaking, and the hills were burning. Even the sky was obliterated by dense clouds which seemed to reflect the anger of the Almighty. A trumpet blown by an unseen angel was filling listeners with dread. Moses was about to meet with the living God and wondered what the outcome would be. Israel had been warned not to approach the mountain, for contact would mean instant death. Israel's leader was walking on a prohibited area, and that was enough to frighten any man. Higher and higher he went, until finally he reached his destination. Not since the days of Adam and Eve had any human been so close to the Creator.

When the Ten Commandments were written or engraved upon slabs of stone, the patriarch received the greatest revelation given to man. The majesty of the Almighty was expressed in the ten rules. If Israel obeyed, they would live and prosper; if they did not, they would suffer and die. Unfortunately, that awesome message has been ignored by mankind. The doctrines of holiness have been dismissed by people who indulge in prohibited practices. The Creator is now considered to be the doting parent of all who ignore His laws. Disgusting acts of immorality are now thought to be trifling weaknesses. Recently over national television, a clergyman said he was proud to be a homosexual and thrilled to know God truly loved and appreciated him. That deluded man would have quite an argument with Paul (see Rom. 1:24–27).

Climbing Mount Carmel with Elijah . . .
The Place of Responsibility

Now therefore send, and gather to me all Israel unto mount Carmel, and the prophets of Baal four hundred and fifty, and the prophets of the groves four hundred, which eat at Jezebel's table (1 Kings 18:19).

All the inhabitants of Israel were filled with apprehension, for a tremendous confrontation was about to take place. King Ahab was infuriated because the meddlesome prophet somehow had changed the weather patterns, and no rain had fallen on the land for over three years. Now that preacher had made an appearance and was about to meet the king. The royal party was already on Mount Carmel. Trouble was anticipated.

And Elijah came unto all the people, and said, How long halt ye between two opinions? If the LORD be God, follow him: but if Baal, then follow him. And the people answered him not a word. . . . And Elijah said unto all the people, Come near unto me. And all the people came near unto him. And he repaired the altar of the LORD that was broken down (1 Kings 18:21, 30).

When the fire fell upon God's altar, Israel was given a revelation from heaven. God alone was capable of supplying the needs of mankind. He could and would, but God and Baal could never occupy the same temple. When Elijah slew the false prophets who had seduced the nation, the people were reminded of God's stern warning: "Thou shalt have no other gods before me." The

41

world needs to remember those words are as valid today as they were when first given to Moses.

Climbing the High Mountain with Christ...
The Place of Resistance

And the devil, taking him [Jesus] up into an high mountain, shewed unto him all the kingdoms of the world in a moment of time. And the devil said unto him, All this power will I give thee, and the glory of them: for that is delivered unto me; and to whomsoever I will give it. If thou therefore wilt worship me, all shall be thine (Luke 4:5–7).

From a lofty place it is possible to see many things, and that was particularly true on the day when Satan and the Savior stood on a high mountain looking through time toward eternity. When the Devil offered to surrender the kingdoms of the world in exchange for an act of worship, he revealed important facts. (1) *He had not changed!* During earth's earliest ages, Lucifer fell from heaven because he desired to be like the Most High (see Isa. 14:12–15), and although centuries brought changes to the world, Satan never lost his original desire. (2) The Devil's claim to be the ruler of the world was never denied by the Lord. Unfortunately, through Adam's folly, the Evil One became the god of this world. It was the purpose of the Savior to redeem mankind, and the insidious temptation presented Christ with a way to avoid the Cross. One act of worship would apparently make the Crucifixion unnecessary. Satan appeared to be generous in his offer, but compliance would have lost forever the opportunity to bring humanity back to God. Sometimes the longest way around is the shortest way home!

Climbing the Mount of Transfiguration with the Disciples...
The Place of Reunion

And it came to pass about eight days after these sayings, he took Peter and John and James, and went up into a mountain to pray. . . . And behold, there talked with him two men, which were Moses and Elias (Luke 9:28, 30).

They had made their choice! Nine disciples had remained in the valley, and were probably enjoying fellowship in the home

42

of a friend. Peter, James, and John would have loved to be among them, but they had accompanied Jesus into the mountain to pray. Luke wrote: "And as he prayed, the fashion of his countenance was altered" (Luke 9:29). The frail barrier of flesh could not hide the eternal glory which Jesus had shared with His Father from before the commencement of time. His face shone with indescribable brilliance, and even His clothes glowed with radiance from His body. That sight could never be forgotten, and many years later, when Peter wrote to his friends, he was still thinking of that memorable experience (see 2 Peter 1:18).

Overcome by weariness the disciples fell asleep, but when they awakened, they saw Moses and Elijah speaking with their Lord. In spite of everything, Moses did enter the Promised Land. God buried only the patriarch's body! Elijah enjoyed a more spectacular entrance; he went home in one of God's chariots of fire. When centuries later they returned to the Promised Land, they brought a special message about the work Christ would accomplish through His death (see Luke 9:31). That meeting on the mountain was only a reunion of friends who had often met in God's country. The patriarch would have smiled to hear Paul explaining that those who die in the Lord were "absent from the body and home with the Lord" (see 2 Cor. 5:8). Moses knew death was dead!

Climbing the Mount of Olives with Jesus...
The Place of Renewal
And it came to pass in those days, that he [Christ] went out into a mountain to pray, and continued all night in prayer to God (Luke 6:12).

And he came out, and went as he was wont to the mount of Olives; and his disciples also followed him (Luke 22:39).

It was not easy for Christ to maintain His daily schedule of activity, for crowds followed Him everywhere. The New Testament records how during a tremendous storm on the Sea of Galilee, Jesus slept. When the winds had whipped the waves to fury, and thunder and lightning shattered the silence of the night, the desperate fishermen feared for their safety. Yet, the Lord lay in a deep sleep until awakened by His followers (see Mark 4:38). There were occasions when the Savior could hardly keep His eyes open; there was no time to relax. How then did He maintain His daily program? The answer to that important question can only be found in the Mount of Olives. That particular hill is not a high mountain. It is one of the smallest in the country, yet it became a sanctuary where, throughout the night, Jesus communed with His Father. During the day people worked there in vineyards and other places, but at night they slept. Probably that was the reason why Jesus waited for darkness to arrive before He went there to pray. He taught: "Men ought always to pray, and not to faint" (Luke 18:1). This was the Lord's method of renewing His strength. Isaiah said: "But they that wait upon the LORD shall renew their strength; they shall mount up with wings as eagles; they shall run, and not be weary; and they shall walk, and not faint" (Isa. 40:31).

Climbing Calvary with Memories . . .
The Place of Redemption

My wife and I, on our twenty-fifth wedding anniversary, slowly walked to the place where the Savior died. At that time it was possible to do so; today special permission must be sought, for that hallowed site is a cemetery. The unpardonable conduct of senseless hippies compelled the Moslem elders to close their burial ground to all outsiders, and today it is only possible to look through large iron gates that exclude foreigners. We stood on the brow of the hill, looked at the tomb in the garden, and knew we were within a short distance of the "Place of a Skull." There, we thanked God for our redemption. Later I took my party of tourists to that same spot, and as they sat in the shade of a tree, we remembered Christ's death. Birds were singing in the trees, but their song could not be compared with the music filling our souls. We were worshiping at the most sacred place on earth.

> Wounded for me, wounded for me,
> There on the cross He was wounded for me;
> Gone my transgressions, and now I am free,
> All because Jesus was wounded for me.

Climbing a Great Mountain with an Angel . . .
The Place of Recognition

Come hither, I will shew thee the bride, the Lamb's wife. And he [the angel] carried me away in the spirit to a great and high mountain, and shewed me that great city, the holy Jerusalem, descending out of heaven from God (Rev. 21:9–10).

It is to be regretted that Revelation is the least understood of all the books of the Bible. The apostle John mentioned four wonderful truths when he wrote his message.

The Lamb's Blood Redeeming (Rev. 5:9)
The Lamb's Bride Rejoicing (Rev. 19:7)
The Lamb's Book Revealing (Rev. 20:12)
The Lamb's Building Remaining (Rev. 21:10–27)

He was amazed to see the greatest city ever constructed slowly descending from heaven. It mattered not how this was accomplished, for although the city was fifteen hundred miles square and fifteen hundred miles high, the laws of gravity were inoperative when the massive structure gracefully descended from the sky. It was the fulfillment of the promise made by the Savior: "Let not your heart be troubled: ye believe in God, believe also in me. In my Father's house are many mansions: if it were not so, I would have told you. *I go to prepare a place for you.* And if I go and prepare a place for you, I will come again and receive you unto myself" (John 14:1–3).

The Celestial City is to be the home of the Bride—the church—where the redeemed will live with Christ eternally. All the types, predictions, and promises of the Scriptures will have been fulfilled, and whatever surprises may await God's people, that glittering city will be at the center of everything. John said: "And the city had no need of the sun, neither of the moon to shine in it, for the glory of God did lighten it, and the Lamb is the light thereof" (Rev. 21:23). That amazing place will be God's everlasting monument to the faithfulness of His Son, whose sacrificial death redeemed sinners. John was taken to a high mountain to see this spectacle, but one day, perhaps soon, we shall enter through the gates to behold the Lamb Himself. The poet was inspired when he wrote:

I have heard of a land on a far away strand,
In the Bible the story is told,

45

Where cares never come, never darkness nor gloom,
And nothing shall ever grow old.

There's a home in that land,
At the Father's right hand
There are mansions whose joys are untold,
And perennial spring, where the birds ever sing,
And nothing shall ever grow old.

In that beautiful land on that far away strand,
No storms with their blasts ever frown.
The streets, I am told, are paved with pure gold,
And the sun, it shall never go down.

DAVID—WHO TRIED TO GET GOD
TO CHANGE HIS MIND

David therefore besought God for the child; and David
fasted, and went in, and lay all night upon the earth. . . . And
it came to pass on the seventh day that the child died (2 Sam.
12:16, 18).

It has been said that God always answers prayer, but sometimes He says no. Most people understand that fact, however,
when sincere prayer does not obtain the desired result, disappointment and doubt often overwhelm the soul. Yet, even when
the Lord says no, that constitutes an answer, although it be nega-
tive. Perhaps one of the outstanding examples of this truth is
found in the experience of David. He prayed day and night and
continued without food for a week, but God refused to grant his
petition. The king was bitterly disappointed, but when his child
died, the nation knew the Almighty had refused to grant the
royal request. Nevertheless, every cloud has its silver lining, and
there is reason to believe that when David ultimately reviewed
the situation, he was compelled to admit (in the poet's words),

> God moves in a mysterious way
> His wonders to perform.

Proposition 1 . . . *God's Glory Is Greater than Man's Gladness*

David was devastated. His love for Bathsheba, the adoration
of the child she had borne, and his disturbed conscience were
creating a situation with which he could not cope. He was
ashamed of his conduct, and the condemnation expressed by the
prophet had deepened his anguish. It was inconceivable that he
had murdered one of his friends to satisfy his own lust. Perhaps
the king for the first time had seen himself.

He remembered the day when he first saw the beautiful
Bathsheba and permitted illicit desires to exist within his soul.
He resembled Esau who sold his birthright for a bowl of carnal
desire. His sin had been unveiled, and every person in the land
was aware of his disgraceful behavior. He, who was a devoted
follower of the Lord, had disgraced his calling and dishonored
God. He asked himself, "How could I have been such a fool?" In

spite of all his conniving, Bathsheba had carried her child, and the helplessness of the baby captivated David's soul. He probably asked, "Why should this little boy suffer for my sin?" and day after day asked the Lord to be merciful. Nathan the prophet had pronounced judgment, saying:

> Now therefore the sword shall never depart from thine house; because thou hast despised me, and hast taken the wife of Uriah the Hittite to be thy wife. . . . Because by this deed thou hast given great occasion to the enemies of the LORD to blaspheme, the child that is born unto thee shall surely die (2 Sam. 12:10–14).

David not only murdered a man and stole his wife; he had brought dishonor upon the name of the Lord. His conduct had offended many critical people. The statement regarding giving an occasion unto the enemies of the Lord was very explicit. There is truth in the lines

> Humpty Dumpty sat on a wall;
> Humpty Dumpty had a great fall.
> All the king's horses
> And all the king's men
> Couldn't put Humpty Dumpty
> Together again.

Unfortunately when an ordinary citizen commits an offense, onlookers shrug their shoulders, but when a prominent servant of God is guilty of a similar offense, everybody condemns him as a hypocrite. If David's crime had only affected himself and his wife, the deed might not have been publicized. Their sinful behavior was as a boulder falling into a pool; repercussions were widespread. Perhaps David considered God's treatment to be harsh and wondered if the Lord were oblivious to human suffering. The baby had become desperately ill, but the king's prayer was ineffective. Was the Lord blind, deaf, and merciless? Perhaps David failed to realize that God was also hurting, but the principles of righteousness had been violated, and people were watching. Had the king's petition been granted, it might have encouraged other people to sacrifice honor on an altar of selfishness.

Moses committed one error, but because of the indiscretion was not permitted to enter Canaan. Throughout history when Hebrew mothers told the story of the great patriarch, when hearts and eyes were filled with wonder, they always concluded by saying, "But Moses was not allowed to enter this land because he disobeyed God." Thus was the nation taught the value of obedience. Similarly, when the subjects of David saw how the Lord dealt with their leader, a warning was written on their consciences. God's glory is more important than anything else in existence, and that might have been one of the reasons why Jesus said, "Seek ye *first* the kingdom of God and his righteousness, and all these things shall be added unto you" (Matt. 6:33).

Proposition 2 . . . *God's Grace Is Greater than Man's Guilt*

And David said unto Nathan, I have sinned against the LORD. And Nathan said unto David, The LORD also hath put away thy sin; thou shalt not die (2 Sam. 12:13).

David had no excuse for his behavior; no argument could justify his conduct. He was guilty and deserved any judgment which the Almighty might decree. Yet it was strange that the Lord put away David's sin even before it was confessed. The grace of God is beyond comprehension; happy is the person who becomes its recipient. Nevertheless it did not free the king from condemnation.

Thus saith the Lord, Behold, I will raise up evil against thee out of thine own house, and I will take thy wives before thine eyes, and give them unto thy neighbour, and he shall lie with thy wives in the sight of this sun. For thou didst it secretly, but I will do this thing before all Israel, and before the sun (2 Sam. 12:11–12).

The apparent leniency of God's mercy was mystifying, for David's repentance could not resurrect his victim. Other men guilty of a similar crime would have been executed. Why should a king be treated differently from an ordinary citizen? How could Jehovah be selective in administrating justice? Paul might have said: "But where sin abounded, grace did much more abound" (Rom. 5:20). He might also have explained how this unpleasant experience

49

unveiled David's true self. The king prayed: "Have mercy upon
me, O God, according to thy lovingkindness: according unto the
multitude of thy tender mercies blot out my transgressions. Wash
me throughly from mine iniquity, and cleanse me from my sin.
For I acknowledge my transgressions: and my sin is ever before
me" (Ps. 51:1–3). Jeremiah would have agreed with the apostle,
for he said: "It is of the LORD's mercies that we are not consumed,
because his compassions fail not. They are new every morning:
great is thy faithfulness" (Lam. 3:22–23). It must be difficult for
God to reject a penitent soul, for He delights in being merciful.
Micah was correct when he wrote: "Who is a God like unto thee
that pardoneth iniquity, and passeth by the transgression of the
remnant of his heritage? He retaineth not his anger forever, because he delighteth in mercy" (Mic. 7:18). Every sincere soul
would agree with the prophet's statement: "It is of the LORD's
mercies that we are not consumed" for "all have sinned, and come
short of the glory of God" (Rom. 3:23).

Proposition 3 . . . *God's Gift Is Greater than Man's Grief*

> And David comforted Bathsheba his wife, and went in unto
> her, and lay with her: and she bore a son, and he called his
> name Solomon: and the LORD loved him (2 Sam. 12:24).

Bathsheba's eyes had become stars reflecting the pleasure of
God. A night of remorse and grief had been followed by a glorious dawn. A baby boy lay in the arms of his adoring mother, and
probably the hosts of heaven were rejoicing. David had been
spared—at least from death; his wife's heart was filled with gratitude, for in some wonderful way, God's anger had been appeased.

It is difficult to decide how much time elapsed between the
death of Bathsheba's first child and the birth of Solomon. A casu-
al reading of 2 Samuel 12:24 might suggest she conceived her
new baby soon after the death of the first, but other Scriptures
suggest another possibility. The *Pulpit Bible* states she might have
had other children before the arrival of Solomon. It is thought that
the delay provided David with an opportunity to demonstrate the
sincerity of his repentance. Many years later it was written:

> And David said to Solomon, My son, as for me, it was in my
> mind to build a house unto the name of the LORD my God:

But the word of the LORD came to me, saying, Thou hast shed blood abundantly, and hast made great wars: thou shalt not build a house unto my name, because thou hast shed much blood upon the earth in my sight. Behold, a son shall be born to thee, who shall be a man of rest; and I will give him rest from all his enemies round about: for his name shall be Solomon, and I will give peace and quietness unto Israel in his days (1 Chron. 22:7–9).

The fact that God instructed David long before the birth of Solomon seems to provide convincing evidence that the king had survived what might be termed a period of probation. This may be debatable, but some facts remain irrefutable.

The Extent of God's Grace

God will pardon any sincere suppliant. "But where sin abounded, grace did much more abound" (Rom. 5:20).

> A welcome is given by Jesus
> To all who will come to His feet.
> And a welcome given by Jesus
> Is wondrously full and complete.
> There's never a man who has wandered
> Past the reach of His wonderful love,
> And never a man who has fallen
> Too low for the mansions above.

The Entreaty of God's Grace

"Come now, and let us reason together, saith the LORD: though your sins be as scarlet, they shall be white as snow; though they be red like crimson, they shall be as wool" (Isa. 1:18). It is better and wiser to kneel at God's feet than to run away and hide.

The Encouragement of God's Grace

When David was overwhelmed by guilt, when his future seemed to be in great danger, and there was no escape from his turmoil, God found a way to solve his problems. He sent a baby to restore David's happiness (see Ps. 51:12). If the mercy of God is so boundless, there is hope for all of us!

51

A TRIP DOWN MEMORY LANE—AS TOLD BY
THE WOMAN OF SHUNEM

My name is of little consequence; it is sufficient to say I was born on a farm in the land of Shunem, and because my parents were moderately wealthy, I enjoyed privileges denied to most of the children who lived in our area. My father and mother were God-fearing people who taught me to respect and serve Jehovah. Naturally, as I grew older, I experienced all the longings familiar to other young ladies, and I secretly prayed that I would find a man so that together we could enjoy our own family. Eventually I met the one who was destined to become my husband, and the fulfillment of my dreams seemed to come a little closer. He was a farmer and acquainted with everything associated with agriculture. When my parents died, I inherited the property, and life took on a new meaning for both of us. I believed in God but apparently something was lacking in my faith. I might say that my beliefs were intellectual; they were in my mind but not in my soul. Now as I look back over the years, four words seem to sum up my experiences. They are: *gratitude, grief, guidance,* and *gladness.*

Perhaps, if I deal with them one at a time and in that order, you will better understand what happened to me.

Gratitude

We were well known in our district, and some of the people referred to me as The Great Woman of Shunem (2 Kings 4:8), but whether or not that definition was earned remains debatable. Perhaps they were referring to my property, which, as I have said, was considerable; however, material possessions, though desirable, cannot satisfy the deepest longings of a woman's soul. My husband and I prayed earnestly that God would favor us with a child, but as the years passed by, it seemed as if our prayers would not be answered. We were extremely disappointed, and slowly our faith began to wane.

And then one day I saw a stranger walking along the dusty road near to our farm. This was unusual, for our neighbors spent most of their time working in the fields. This man of distinction had a servant who appeared to be very respectful. Yet the man himself was different. At first I did not take much notice, but when he continued at intervals to return, I began to wonder why he was coming and what was his mission. I remember saying to my husband: "Behold now, I perceive that this is an holy man of God, which passeth by us continually. Let us make a little chamber, I pray thee, on the wall; and let us set for him there a bed, and a table, and a stool, and a candlestick: and it shall be, when he cometh to us, that he shall turn in thither" (2 Kings 4:9–10). We were both captivated and looked forward eagerly to his arrival. Our house soon became a rest-home on the highway. We discovered he was a prophet called Elisha. He often spoke about his former master, Elijah, who had recently gone home to heaven. When in the evening he spoke to us, my husband and I were fascinated, for he told amazing stories. We were filled with regret when he ceased. We could have listened to him forever.

Then came the morning when I had the shock of my life. Gehazi, the prophet's servant, told me his master wished to see me. Rather nervously I went to stand in the doorway of his room. He looked at me and said: "About this season, according to the time of life, thou shalt embrace a son." I was completely astonished and could only whisper, "Nay, my lord, thou man of God, do not lie unto thine handmaid." Afterward I seemed to be walking on air; the impossible was happening, and as the months passed, my body told me that I was not dreaming. Perhaps it was at that time the God of my intellect became the Lord of my heart. Often in the great crises of life, this happens to people. Perhaps it will not seem amiss if I ask my listeners if this ever happened to them.

Grief

The years began to pass, my baby became an attractive boy and was the joy of my life. I had to be his mother, teacher, friend, and guide, but every day was a little bit of heaven on earth. God had been gracious to me, and my child seemed to be a small angel sent down to dispel my loneliness. At harvest time he loved to accompany his father into the fields, and the servants loved him as he tried to emulate their example. No music could compare with my boy's laughter. Little did I know when one morning I packed his lunch, that the day was to be the darkest of my life. Storm clouds were about to eclipse the sun! Out in the fields my son was trying to help the men when, placing his hands to his head, he cried, "My head, my head." My husband, who did not realize the seriousness of the situation, said to a lad, "Carry him to his mother." When I saw the fellow carrying the limp form in his arms, my heart stood still. I hardly knew what I was doing, but somehow I carried my son up to the prophet's chamber and laid him on the bed. Then I went out and shut the door. I continued to ask myself, "Why did God give him to me if He intended to take him so soon?" I had no answer, but nothing else mattered at that moment. I had needed God in life; I needed Him much more in death. Now as I remember that terrible moment, it seems as an awful nightmare. I sought and found Elisha, and eventually he arrived at my home, and I watched as he ascended the stairs to his chamber. I did not know all that took place until I was informed later by the servant. I heard the prophet's footsteps as he walked to and fro, and realized that even he was fighting a great battle, that his soul was also filled with anguish. Then suddenly I heard my child sneezing, as if he were catching a cold.

I did not fully comprehend all that was taking place, but when the door opened, I saw the servant smiling. He invited me to enter the chamber, and when I did, I saw the prophet standing alongside the bed. He said, "Take up thy son." I could hardly move. My feet seemed fastened to the floor, but there stood my boy as if he had just awakened from sleep. I wanted to rush over and hug him, but something prevented me. The prophet was gravely watching. Perhaps he was wondering what my reactions would be. Instinctively, I went over and fell at his feet to whisper, "Thank you." Then I took up my boy and went down to my kitchen. Tears were streaming down my face as I hugged him. I wonder now if Jehovah was smiling. What might have happened had I neglected to go to the prophet?

> Prayer is the soul's sincere desire;
> Uttered or unexpressed;
> The motion of a hidden fire,
> That trembles in the breast.

Guidance

I smile now when I read the account supplied by the ancient writer.

Then spake Elisha unto the woman, whose son he had restored to life, saying Arise, and go thou and thine household, and sojourn wheresoever thou canst sojourn: for the Lord hath called for a famine; and it shall also come upon the land seven years (2 Kings 8:1).

I cannot help but wonder if people ever realize what happened on that fateful morning when I saw Elisha approaching my home. I had not forgotten the miracle that restored my son to me, but this special visit from the prophet was unexpected. After my husband's death, my son and I, with the help of God, had continued to farm the land and were content. When Elisha commanded me to leave my property and hurry to an unknown destination, I was dumbfounded. We had worked so hard to maintain the farm, and to leave everything at a moment's notice seemed unreasonable. But I already knew that Elisha was a man of God who was the messenger of the Almighty. He urged us to hurry as there was no time to lose. I quickly gathered things essential for the journey, sold what equipment was possible, and with any money I could obtain, sadly left our property. This was not easy for that farm was the dearest place on earth. Where could we go? What could be done when we arrived? What would happen to my son if I died in a strange land? What would your reactions be if you were placed in a similar position?

When we arrived in the land of the Philistines, we made a few inquiries and eventually settled in a small village. At first everything appeared to be bewildering, but fortunately we had sufficient funds to meet our daily needs. I do not think my son understood all that was happening, but I was determined he would never forget his homeland. Each night I told him stories about our native land, but after he went to sleep, I sat and sometimes wept. What had happened to my farm? Were other people living there and working the land? Had we already been forgotten? Yes, I knew God had brought us to this foreign land, but would He ever take us home again?

That first year was terrible; the next was almost as bad, but after that, my grief was not so intense. When I saw my new neighbors reaping their harvest, my heart missed a beat, and my memories became intensely active. I wondered if Jehovah had forgotten me. That was an awful feeling. My sisters, did you ever have a similar experience? As darkness enveloped my soul, I began to wonder if the sun would ever shine again. The psalmist asked himself: "Why art thou cast down, O my soul?" but then he said: "Hope thou in God for I shall yet praise Him" (Ps. 42:5).

Yes, I am truly traveling down memory's lane when I recall that after seven years, I heard God whispering: "It's time to go home."

> And it came to pass at the seven years' end, that the woman returned out of the land of the Philistines: and she went forth to cry unto the king for her house and for her land (2 Kings 8:3).

The day had arrived, and I did not care what danger lay ahead. I had learned that a crust of bread in my homeland was better than a banquet in a foreign land. My boy and I had to travel over a hundred miles to reach our country, and the journey was not an easy one. Most of our money had been spent, and our financial security was at an all-time low. We were at the end of our resources and completely dependent upon the Lord. It was impossible for us to know that each step was counted by God, and He controlled everything. We did not know then that our arrival had already been arranged. We could neither arrive late, nor early. Our problem was only a part of a jigsaw puzzle which the Almighty was patiently putting together. As we reviewed the entire episode, we became convinced God is too wise to make a mistake, and too loving to be unkind. Jehovah was calmly calculating every phase of our long journey.

When we entered our homeland, what would be the best thing to do? To proceed to our former home would be unwise, for other people would be living there. To go elsewhere would be impossible, for we had little if any money to buy or rent a new home. To appeal to a local magistrate would be useless; people who left Israel to live among Philistines would never be popular and certainly not compensated for losses. I soon realized that an appeal to the king was my only hope of securing assistance. Perhaps when I decided to approach the ruler, God smiled. Life teaches how the just shall live by faith; men and women must proceed even when the road ahead seems uninviting. There is always help just around the corner.

Gladness

I was surprised when I saw the king seated in the open air and speaking loudly to a beggar who was standing a small distance away. I wondered if it would be wise to interrupt the proceedings, for oftentimes kings have ruthless ways of dealing with offenders. I was unaware of events which had taken place during my stay in Philistia; I did not know that the servant of Elisha had become a leper and had been banished to a place of isolation. Neither did I know that the king, who was not known for piety, had developed a keen interest in the exploits of a prophet who had formerly been despised. For some inexplicable reason, the monarch desired to know more about Elisha, and when he heard Gehazi could provide information, he threw caution to the winds and summoned the doomed man into his presence.

He asked the leper if he could supply what he needed to hear, and receiving an affirmative reply, commanded the fellow to tell a story about his former master. When my son and I arrived, the man was actually telling the king about us, and to say the least, I was astonished. There were many amazing stories which could be told about Elisha, but for some inscrutable reason, on the spur of the moment, the informant began to describe how Elisha restored life to my boy. I thought this was an opportune moment and cried: "O King, please help me." Surprised, the monarch turned his head to look at me; the leper ceased speaking; there was a moment of silence, and then the leper shouted: "My Lord, O king, this is the woman, and this is her son, whom Elisha restored to life" (2 Kings 8:5). For a few moments everyone appeared to be confused. The king was trying to understand the situation, the leper was staring at me and the boy, and the silence was deafening! Then the king asked if the story was true and where I had been, etc.

When I had told the story how God had commanded me to leave the land so that the approaching famine would not deprive us of sustenance, the king said to an officer: "Restore all that was hers, and all the fruit of the field, since the day that she left the land, even until now." As I listened I did not know whether to laugh or cry. Probably the tenant to be evicted was also compensated, but there could never be a happier day than that we experienced when once again we walked around our newly acquired property. It is still difficult to believe that God paid for our seven-year vacation in a foreign land. He surely knew how to honor His word and care for His dependents. I have truly escorted you down my memory lane, and in so doing have enriched my soul. What can I say in conclusion? Perhaps David says it best:

I have been young, and now am old; yet have I not seen the righteous forsaken, nor his seed begging bread (Ps. 37:25).

My journey into the past seems to proclaim a great truth: *It pays to trust in the living God.*

And next unto him repaired Shallum the son of Halohesh, the ruler of the half part of Jerusalem, he and his daughters (Neh. 3:12).

The text is unusual and thought-provoking. It appeared that Nehemiah's Hall of Fame was reserved exclusively for males, but suddenly among many builders, the daughters of a ruler were seen working side by side with men. The total number of workmen is unknown. For example, it is written "the men of Jericho" repaired one section of the wall, and Nehemiah did not specify how many of those citizens participated. Evidently there were hundreds and possibly thousands of workmen, for the area covered was immense. The entire wall was being repaired at the same time. When news circulated through the country that Nehemiah had arrived from Babylon with authority to help the Jews, volunteers came from all parts of the land and there were many laborers.

The history recorded in the book of Nehemiah is one of the most exciting accounts in the Scriptures. His secret examination of the ruins of the city and the subsequent meeting with the elders reveal the secrecy with which the initial preparation was made. When builders and the materials were available, Nehemiah and his counselors assigned workers to their various places, and suddenly around the wall intense activity began. Rubbish was removed, foundations were laid or repaired, and the sounds of hammers and chisels falling upon stone could be heard everywhere. When determined men rolled up their sleeves and commenced their colossal task, it was surprising, to say the least, when one of the two rulers of the city brought his work-party of daughters. They were the only females accepted by Nehemiah, and although for reasons unknown their names were not included in the city's hall of fame, they worked unceasingly with the men and earned for themselves an abiding place in the affections of all who love Jerusalem.

The twentieth century has many halls of fame. Athletes from every sport are chosen to receive awards of merit, but ladies are never welcomed in places reserved for men. During ancient history this fact was even more pronounced, for women were considered to be inferior citizens. They worked in the fields, prepared meals, and produced children. To discover them working side by side with men was unprecedented.

The Daughters Who Worked

It is difficult to decide the type of task they performed. Every visitor to Jerusalem knows the immense size of the stone blocks used in ancient constructions. It is still uncertain how the pyramids in Egypt were erected. Some scholars believe the huge stones were rolled on timber upon banks of earth to positions far above the ground. Others believe these monuments were only made possible by techniques brought from distant planets. It is quite evident that women could not handle such huge blocks of masonry. Maybe they supervised the making of mortar or slime, or perhaps served as messengers for Nehemiah as he communicated with foremen around the walls. Their presence revealed a determination to do everything possible in restoring the city of God. While time continues, these women of a bygone era will be remembered with gratitude, for they "being dead, yet speak" (see Heb. 11:4).

It is possible that in one way or another many women helped in the reconstruction of the walls of Jerusalem. There was always the possibility of enemy attacks, and it was necessary for builders to defend their work.

> They which builded on the wall, and they that bare burdens, with those that laded, every one with one of his hands wrought in the work, and with the other hand held a weapon. For the builders, every one had his sword girded by his side, and so builded. And he that sounded the trumpet was by me (Neh. 4:17–18).

The men on the walls had to be fed, and there remains the possibility that a great company of women prepared meals for their husbands and sons and made sure the workmen would never be hungry. Without such assistance the walls would not have been completed. Nevertheless, the question remains, why were the daughters of Shallum mentioned by Nehemiah when other women were ignored? There had to be some outstanding service rendered by these ladies. That civic official could have found

60

less arduous tasks for his girls, such as working in administrative offices where there was no danger. Those brave women resemble others of our modern world who are not content to sit in an office when they can be with men in the trenches!

The Daughters Who Witnessed

And we entered into the house of Philip the evangelist, which was one of the seven, and abode with him. And the same man had four daughters, virgins, which did prophesy (Acts 21:8–9).

Philip the evangelist was one of the best known men in the early church. At a time of crisis he was appointed by the apostles to help in overseeing the needs of impoverished people (see Acts 6:5). Later, he conducted a successful evangelistic crusade in Samaria (see Acts 8:5) and was sent to the desert to intercept an Ethiopian dignitary returning to his country after attending a feast in Jerusalem (see Acts 8:26–40).

It would seem that like Shallum who helped to rebuild the walls of Jerusalem, Philip had no sons, but he was the father of four daughters who were the joy of his life. Women worked within the church, but they were not encouraged to become public speakers. It was thought advisable that they remain silent in the assemblies (see 1 Cor. 14:34). It was therefore significant when the daughters of Philip were anointed by the Holy Spirit to become prophetesses—tellers forth—of the good news of the Gospel. There is no evidence that they preached or prophesied in the services, but, on the other hand, there is nothing to prove they did not. God's servants ministered when they were "moved by the Holy Spirit," and not when they decided to make a speech! These women could not have been old, for the fact their father was appointed to be an administrator suggests he was a man about forty or fifty years of age. His girls, therefore, would have been in their late twenties. They had never been married, and as far as is known, had no desire to be; they belonged to Christ. Whether or not they helped their father in his crusades is not known. If they did, Philip was a very fortunate man. His success as an administrator and preacher was probably due, in part, to inspiration received from his daughters.

Philip must have owned a large house in Caesarea, for when Paul and his companions arrived in the city, they "entered into

61

the house of Philip the evangelist, which was one of the seven, *and abode with him.*" The daughters were delighted to entertain such a distinguished guest, and having male company in the house was a delightful change. Their concern deepened when they became aware of Paul's intention to attend the forthcoming festival in Jerusalem, and their fears increased when a prophet named Agabus arrived to warn him of impending disaster. Luke, describing what followed, said: "And when we heard these things, both we, and they of that place, besought him [Paul] not to go up to Jerusalem" (Acts 21:12). They were in the home of Philip, so the statement "they of that place" could only mean Philip and his daughters. The advice given was rejected, for the apostle was determined to please himself. Unfortunately, his decision result-ed in two years imprisonment, when he might have been leading souls to Christ.

It has been said that behind every successful man stands a woman. Philip was very fortunate, for he had the continuing support of four delightful daughters who earned an abiding place in God's Hall of Fame. It would be nice if we knew their names, but perhaps getting to know them will be one of the joys to be experienced in eternity.

The Daughters Who Worshiped

Then Jesus six days before the passover came to Bethany, where Lazarus was which had been dead, whom he raised from the dead. There they made him a supper; and Martha served: but Lazarus was one of them that sat at the table with him. Then took Mary a pound of ointment of spikenard, very costly, and anointed the feet of Jesus, and wiped his feet with her hair: and the house was filled with the odour of the oint-ment (John 12:1–3).

Mary and Martha of Bethany were sisters, but who was their father? Tradition says they were the daughters of Simon the leper. Whether or not this report is accurate is open to conjec-ture. It has been affirmed that Simon had been a leper cleansed by Jesus. To distinguish him from other Simons, he retained his old name which reminded him of the debt owed to his bene-factor. His desire to entertain the Lord was an outpouring of love and gratitude. His separate house may have preserved his independence. All this is conjecture, but Martha, Mary, and Lazarus were close friends of Simon. Whoever the father might have been, he had every reason to be proud of his daughters who became two of the best loved Bible characters.

Martha was industrious, but Mary was contemplative—a dreamer—easily lost in her thoughts. Lazarus was probably a mixture of both. There is no record of anything he said. Martha was easily annoyed; Mary could be provocative. It would be easy to criticize all three of them, but it was significant that after one gentle rebuke given by Jesus, everything changed. Ultimately, the women understood that Jesus was the Son of God and in every way possible worshiped Him. There was never need to rebuke Martha the second time, for during the supper given by Simon she served without complaint (John 12:2). Mary once again was missing when work needed to be done, but when she sacrificed her treasure by pouring the precious ointment on the Lord, Martha probably understood and smiled. Blessed are they who learn important lessons quickly.

As we review these characters from the Bible, we are reminded of three steps to immortality. The daughters of Shallum worked; the daughters of Philip witnessed; the daughters of some unknown father worshiped and became so famous the world now appreciates their adoration of the Son of God. Some people are so busy building walls, they have no time to sit at the feet of the Savior! Others are so anxious to be seen and heard, they are unwilling to become servants in obscure places. Many people would prefer to be chief in a small village, than to be second in an empire. Blessed is the soul who graduates from God's school with honors in work, witnessing, and worship. These are the folk who become successful in time and rewarded in eternity.

*And the L*ORD *God planted a garden eastward in Eden
(Gen. 2:8).*

Beautiful gardens are always attractive, and each year the
nations of the world spend enormous sums of money surrounding their tourist centers with scenes of loveliness. This has always been the case, for even in Bible times kings delighted in
planning royal gardens. Probably one of the most famous was
made by King Ahasuerus of Persia. In the third year of his reign
he invited many international dignitaries to be his guests at a
magnificent party that lasted for one hundred and eighty days.
This illustrious event came to a climax with a special banquet
that lasted intermittently for seven days in "the court of the
garden of the king's palace" (see Est. 1:3–5). The ancient writer
who described that glittering occasion seemed to be ecstatic when
he wrote:

Where were white, green, and blue hangings, fastened with
cords of fine linen and purple to silver rings and pillars of
marble: the beds were of gold and silver, upon a pavement of
red, and blue, and white and black, marble (Est. 1:6).

When interspersed with beds of glorious flowers, that garden
would have graced heaven itself! Perhaps the king arranged for
his plants and flowers to be in pots so that throughout his festivi-
ties ailing plants could be replaced. The magnificent splendor
continued until the day his guests departed. The Bible reveals
that sin commenced in the Garden of Eden; it was challenged in
the Garden of Gethsemane and conquered in the garden where
Christ rose from His tomb. (See also *Bible Highways.*[1]) Much
may be said about the gardens mentioned by ancient writers.

Personally Desired . . . *Wanted*

"And the Lord planted a garden eastward in Eden." I wish I
could have seen that garden. Alas, I was born too late! Did it
possess long winding paths, and were there enchanting borders
of multicolored flowers? Were there shady corners where
Adam sat listening to the songs of the birds? Were some of the

flowering trees aflame with the Creator's art? And did the gentle breezes of evening produce music of exquisite sweetness as they played among the leaves? Yes, I wish I could have seen that garden, for it has been said, "One is nearer to God in a garden than anywhere else on earth." A garden is a mirror reflecting a world. There, we find enemies; there, we find friends. Within the confines of a garden stalks the shadow of death, but in that same shadow may be found promise of glorious resurrection. The gardens of the Bible have a wonderful story to tell.[2]

It appears to be significant that although God *created* the heaven and earth, He *planted* the first garden. Behold God on His knees—possibly with soiled hands! When He brought the worlds into being, would it not have been easy to include a garden with the finest expressions of eternal beauty? The mountain ranges, far reaching forests, the graceful rivers and meadows would have been wonderful settings in which to create a place of outstanding loveliness. The Lord specially designed that garden in Eden. He created the seeds, but it was with love and tenderness He handled the young plants, placing each one exactly where He desired it to be.

The Almighty loved to walk there in the cool of the evening. It was meant to be a sanctuary where He could commune with Adam and Eve. That garden exhibited everything valued by the Creator. He could have commissioned angels to plant it, but that was unsatisfactory. "The LORD God planted a garden. . . . And a river went out of Eden to water the garden" (Gen. 2:8, 10). "And God saw that it was good." When the Lord sat on the banks of that delightful river, did He look down the corridors of time to see gardens of another type? As time progressed, Eden became a memory. Jehovah planned to place other gardens within redeemed hearts, where in the stillness of the human spirit He would commune with those He loved. Yes, He wanted that place in Eden, and He still does within the souls of men and women.

Proudly Displayed . . . *Watered*

When the king of Persia planted his magnificent garden, he arranged that it would be near the canals fed by the river Euphrates. He reigned over the eastern world, and therefore could bring precious commodities from conquered domains. The "red and blue, and white, and black marble" were probably imported

65

items, but with great care each piece was cut and placed into position. The view of the royal garden was amazing. At enormous expense the monarch did everything possible to make the area the most attractive place known to men. When his guests arrived, he proudly escorted them along the winding paths and indicated the prized plants and shrubs. His spirits rose when words of appreciation were spoken; he had produced something unequaled anywhere.

It may be possible to detect that kind of pride in the heart of the Almighty. The Lord had a servant called Job whose heart was a garden that pleased Jehovah. The sacred writings describe how God said to Satan: "Hast thou considered my servant Job, that there is none like him in the earth, a perfect and an upright man, one that feareth God and escheweth evil?" (Job 1:8). God had created a garden within the soul of His servant, and it surpassed anything seen in Eden. Evidently the Lord was intensely proud of that ancient saint. When the faithfulness of Job was questioned by Satan, the Lord permitted his testing because His child was completely reliable, and would withstand every challenge brought against him. The Savior said: "I do always those things that please him" (John 8:29), and that testimony was endorsed when God spoke from heaven saying: "This is my beloved Son, in whom I am well pleased; hear ye him" (Matt. 17:5). When the Almighty looked into the life of Jesus, He saw beauty which made the Garden of Eden fade into insignificance.

Perceptively Damaged . . . *Watched*

But the gate of the fountain repaired Shallun the son of Colhozeh, the ruler of part of Mizpeh; he built it and covered it, and set up the doors thereof, the locks thereof, and the bars thereof, and the wall of the pool of Siloah, by the king's garden, and unto the stairs that go down from the city of David (Neh. 3:15).

The kings of Israel and Judah arranged that their special garden would be close to the pool of Siloam, where its seclusion would be an asset. Apparently there was a secret gate in the wall, possibly hidden by ivy or some other shrub. When danger threatened the life of Ahaziah, he fled through that gate but, unfortunately, was overtaken by Jehu who refused to spare the

66

life of the monarch (2 Kings 9:27). After the Babylonian captivity Ezra and Nehemiah returned to their homeland to discover seventy years of decay and neglect had destroyed everything of value, and the task of reconstruction would be immense. The son of a ruler was either assigned, or volunteered, to repair the wall close to what had been the king's garden. It is refreshing to know that this builder was not an ordinary peasant. It is said he was the son of a man who was co-ruler of Mizpeh. Family influence might have found a less arduous task, but evidently the man desired to restore that part of the wall. The king's garden had been neglected but Shallun desired to restore its former grandeur.

Unfortunately there were, and still are, enemies who would destroy everything valued by the King of Kings. They include foes from without and complacency from within. Any believer who would preserve the Savior's property must be ready to work with one hand, and fight with the other. God's enemies are ruthless and sometimes attack when least expected (compare Neh. 4:17–18).

Perpetually Demanding . . . *Work*

Without careful attention any garden can become a wilderness. Evidently King Solomon had seen this happen, for he wrote:

> I went by the field of the slothful, and by the vineyard of the man void of understanding. And, lo, it was all grown over with thorns, and nettles had covered the face thereof, and the stone wall thereof was broken down. Then I saw, and considered it well: I looked upon it, and received instruction. Yet a little sleep, a little slumber, a little folding of the hands to sleep: So shall thy poverty come as one that travelleth; and thy want as an armed man (Prov. 24:30–34).

It is not known how long Adam resided in the Garden of Eden, but one fact is indisputable. God planted the garden, but man was expected to do the weeding![3] "The vineyard of a man void of understanding." That statement described a person whose brain was inactive! Either the man had inherited property or had purchased it. He loved to look at his vineyard but was too tired to work! He loved to dream about possibilities, but while he did, the weeds and thistles increased, and the land became

67

unproductive. Solomon might have learned more from that sleeping husbandman. He described the folly of the dreamer but neglected his own weeding. He who had been given special wisdom permitted Egyptian weeds to grow in his garden, which, within a short time, became inundated with thistles.

But king Solomon loved many strange women, together with the daughter of Pharaoh, women of the Moabites, Ammonites, Edomites, Zidonians, and Hittites. Of the nations concerning which the LORD said unto the children of Israel, Ye shall not go in to them, neither shall they come in unto you: for surely they will turn away your heart after their gods: Solomon clave unto these in love. And he had seven hundred wives, princesses, and three hundred concubines; and his wives turned away his heart (1 Kings 11:1–3).

Solomon proved that the higher a man climbs, the farther he has to fall. He who offered advice through his poems and sonnets became a man "void of understanding." He had a wonderful vineyard, but instead of soiling his hands weeding, he contaminated his soul with infamous conduct.

Perfectly Delightful . . . *Wonderful*

Thus saith the Lord GOD; In the day that I shall have cleansed you from all your iniquities I will also cause you to dwell in the cities, and the wastes shall be builded. And the desolate land shall be tilled, whereas it lay desolate in the sight of all that passed by. And they shall say, This land that was desolate is become like the garden of Eden; and the waste and desolate and ruined cities are become fenced, and are inhabited. Then the heathen that are left round about you shall know that I the Lord build the ruined places, and plant that that was desolate: I the LORD have spoken it, and I will do it (Ezek. 36:33–36).

It is thrilling to know that as the Lord planted a garden in Eden, He intends to do it again but on a much larger scale. Ezekiel spoke of the final days of time when the kingdom of God will be established upon the earth. A foreshadowing of what is to come was supplied when the Hebrews returned from

Babylon. Yet, the details given by the prophet can only be fulfilled when "the earth shall be filled with the glory of the Lord as the waters cover the sea." Then Israel will be transformed into far-reaching places of beauty, and the entire landscape will resemble the garden of God. God said "I will do it."

The coronation of the King of Kings will make all this possible. Wilderness areas should not exist within the life of the Christian. The Lord gave a remarkable promise to His people. "And the Lord shall guide thee continually, and satisfy thy soul in drought, and make fat thy bones; and thou shalt be like a watered garden, and like a spring of water, whose waters fail not" (Isa. 58:11). God is able to make the human heart into a garden filled with rare beauty. Happy is the man or woman who can say:

> I come to the garden alone,
> While the dew is still on the roses;
> And the voice I hear, falling on mine ear,
> The Son of God discloses.
>
> He speaks, and the sound of His voice
> Is so sweet the birds hush their singing;
> And the melody that He gives to me
> Within my heart is ringing.
>
> And He walks with me, and He talks with me,
> And He tells me I am His own;
> And the joy we share as we tarry there
> None other has ever known.
>
> J. Austin Miles

1. Ivor Powell, *Bible Highways* (Grand Rapids: Kregel Publications, 1985), 1.

2. Ibid.

3. Ivor Powell, *Bible Treasures,* (Grand Rapids: Kregel Publications, 1984), 47–48.

JOB—WHO SAW LIGHT
AT THE END OF HIS TUNNEL

For I know that my redeemer liveth, and that he shall stand at
the latter day upon the earth: and though after my skin worms
destroy this body; yet in my flesh shall I see God; Whom I shall
see for myself, and mine eyes shall behold, and not another;
Though my reins be consumed within me (Job 19:25–27).

The eleventh chapter of Hebrews is the Christian's Art Gallery
of Faith. The writer of this remarkable letter was evidently a Jew
who was well acquainted with the tabernacle and temple ritual. He
was a dedicated Christian who saw in the ancient writings promises fulfilled in Christ. The letter was scholarly, illuminating, and
practical. He was aware of the skepticism that prevailed among
Jews and endeavored to prove that without faith it is impossible to
please God. To support that conclusion, he compiled a list of
national ancestors whose faith in Jehovah was outstanding. He
explained that although the patriots were limited in their knowledge, they found happiness in believing. They had faith in God,
accepted His promises, and courageously lived and died in the
confidence that the Lord was still on His throne.

The author's list of celebrities was remarkable. He mentioned
Abel, Enoch, Noah, Abraham, Sarah, Jacob, Joseph, Moses, and
others. Finally when he was running out of time and space on his
manuscript, he said: "And what shall I more say? For the time
would fail me to tell of Gideon, and of Barak, and of Samson, and
of Jephthae; of David also, and Samuel, and of the prophets"
(Heb. 11:32). The list of important people is tremendous, but this
author at least wishes another name had been included. The writer
of this epistle never mentioned Job, who saw light at the end of a
long tunnel of darkness and gloom. That strange but inspiring man
had more faith than many others. His vision of the future was
amazing; his words became immortal. Many biblical celebrities
left nothing to posterity, but every Easter the words of the patriarch are heard around the world. "I know that my Redeemer liveth,
and that he shall stand at the latter day upon the earth." That
statement will never lose its charm.

When the writer to the Hebrews summarized the accomplishments of the Old Testament believers, he said: "These all died in

faith, not having received the promises, but having seen them afar off, and were persuaded of them, and embraced them, and confessed that they were strangers and pilgrims on the earth" (Heb. 11:13). A stranger is a person away from home; a pilgrim is one on a journey to a beloved place! "He [Abraham] looked for a city whose builder and maker was God" (Heb. 11:10). "For they that say such things declare plainly that they seek a country. And truly, if they had been mindful of that country from whence they came out, they might have had opportunity to have returned. But now they desire a better country, that is, an heavenly: wherefore God is not ashamed to be called their God: for he hath prepared for them a city" (Heb. 11:14–16). Abraham looked for a city built by God, but the Lord not only built a city, He also prepared a country.

Unlike those wonderful people, Job apparently did not see everything, but he understood some things equally important. He saw that the Redeemer would come to this world, and by the miracle of redemption Job would see God. That would be a privilege never given to any other Old Testament believer. When Moses climbed Mount Sinai to receive the Ten Commandments, he was allowed to see God's back as Jehovah passed by, but Job understood and emphasized that with *his own eyes* he would behold the Almighty. That amazing man saw four wonderful facts.

He Saw the Worth of a Soul . . . *Remarkable*

My kinsfolk have failed, and my familiar friends have forgotten me. They that dwelt in mine house, and my maids, count me for a stranger: I am an alien in their sight. I called my servant, and he gave me no answer; I intreated him with my mouth. My breath is strange to my wife, though I intreated for the children's sake of mine own body. Yea, young children despised me; I arose, and they spake against me. All my inward friends abhorred me: and they whom I loved are turned against me. My bone cleaveth to my skin and to my flesh, and I am escaped with the skin of my teeth. Have pity upon me, have pity upon me, O ye my friends; for the hand of God hath touched me (Job 19:14–21).

Job's physical condition was terrible to behold; most men in his position would have welcomed death. The once-prominent citizen had become a feeble pauper. His family and friends

71

despised him. His appearance was appalling, for he was nothing but skin and bones, and his body was covered with boils and carbuncles. It was difficult to lie on a bed. Doctors could not alleviate his suffering, and no one could remove the pain from his soul. His body emitted an offensive odor. His breath was sickening, and everybody believed it would be best if he died.

Nevertheless, one fact supplied comfort. There was apparently no hope of his recovery, but he looked into the future and saw a Friend. Job said, "I know that *my* redeemer liveth." Hebrew law permitted a kinsman to redeem any enslaved relative, but redemption was not obligatory. If the slave were worthless, his family could be indifferent, and allow him to remain in bondage. Boaz could not redeem Ruth until another man refused to exercise his prior claim. *A desire to redeem* had to be the compelling circumstance motivating action. It was significant that Job believed he was still valuable in the sight of God, for otherwise the Lord would not be interested in redeeming a useless slave. The poor man referred to *my redeemer*. He believed that God was still concerned about him. Even if he were a sick, friendless old man, God could redeem him for future service. When earthly friends could not or would not help, the Almighty would respond to his need. That message should provide comfort for desperate people everywhere.

Some oppressed souls have been overwhelmed by circumstances beyond their control; others contributed to their own downfall. But even when people are repulsive, God considers them to be of more value than the whole world.

He Saw the Work of the Savior . . . *Redemption*

The exact period in which Job lived is unknown, but it must be significant that he did not refer to his helper as "God," nor did he mention "Jehovah." He said *my redeemer*, and that implied he was seeing light at the end of his tunnel of misery. Any person wishing to redeem someone had to belong to the slave's family. The Redeemer had to come to the slave owner and pay whatever was necessary. Later, in Jewish law he was required to stand in the presence of elders, pay the price of redemption, and, removing a shoe, throw it over his shoulder as evidence the transaction had been completed.

It would be informative if we knew how the patriarch learned such truth. Apparently there was not a prophet during Job's

lifetime, and no temple in which people could seek enlighten-
ment. Yet, in some mysterious manner, Job discovered amazing
truth. God, who lived in the sky, would become human, come to
earth, and pay whatever was necessary to redeem a sinner. Would
it be correct to suggest that this man was the first human ever to
possess such wisdom? Long afterward the apostle Peter wrote:
"Ye were not redeemed with corruptible things, as silver and
gold . . . but with the precious blood of Christ, as of a lamb
without blemish and without spot" (1 Peter 1:18–19).

He Saw the Wonder of Salvation . . . *Resurrection*

> And though . . . worms destroy this body, yet in my flesh
> shall I see God (Job 19:26).

When Job uttered these words, he did not know God was about
to remove the infirmity and restore what had been lost. His body
was a mass of corruption, and there was no hope of recovery. It was
in the darkest hour of his life that Job said: "Though worms destroy
this body, yet in my flesh shall I see God." Had he said: "Though
worms destroy this body, I shall see God," he would have expressed
the belief that somewhere beyond the grave his spirit would behold
the Almighty. When he said: *In my flesh*, he implied that in spite of
the continued deterioration of his health, the Redeemer would supply a new body which would be incorruptible and immortal. Job
believed the Lord would stand upon the earth *in the latter day*.
Possibly he understood that God would be the Savior. Worms destroyed Job's first body, but nothing would disfigure, hurt, or defile
that new body in which he would live eternally. Paul and Job would
have enjoyed discussing these facts, for Paul wrote:

> Behold I shew you a mystery; We shall not all sleep, but we
> shall all be changed. In a moment, in the twinkling of an eye,
> at the last trump: for the trumpet shall sound, and the dead
> shall be raised incorruptible, and we shall be changed. For
> this corruptible must put on incorruption, and this mortal must
> put on immortality. So when this corruptible shall have put on
> incorruption, and this mortal shall have put on immortality,
> then shall be brought to pass the saying that is written, Death
> is swallowed up in victory. O death, where is thy sting? O
> grave, where is thy victory? (1 Cor. 15:51–55).

He Saw the Worship of a Saint . . . *Recognition*

Yet in my flesh, shall I see God; whom I shall see for myself, and mine eyes shall behold, and not another (Job 19:26–27).

And they shall see his face; and his name shall be in their foreheads (Rev. 22:4).

Philip saith unto him, Lord, shew us the Father and it sufficeth us. Jesus saith unto him, Have I been so long time with you, and yet hast thou not known me, Philip? he that hath seen me hath seen the Father; and how sayest thou then, Shew us the Father? Believest thou not that I am in the Father, and the Father in me? the words that I speak unto you I speak not of myself: but the Father that dwelleth in me, he doeth the works (John 14:8–10).

Man's relationship with the Almighty has always been mystical. God walked in the Garden of Eden because He desired fellowship with Adam and Eve. Unfortunately they were expelled from the area. Later, when the cloud and fire hovered over the tabernacle, Israel knew Jehovah was in the vicinity. Centuries later Jesus called and ordained disciples who never understood how to enjoy fellowship with God. Philip expressed the thoughts of his colleagues when he asked Jesus to reveal the Father. The Lord's reply was clear and convincing: "Philip, if you desire to see the Father, look at Me. If you wish to hear His word, listen to me. I am the Father walking among you, talking with you, and loving you as any father would love his children."

Throughout the remaining part of their lives those men believed God had lived among them, and their greatest hope was that soon they would see Him again. John described how Christians, having reached their eternal home, would "see his face." He also wrote how "the four and twenty elders fell down and worshiped him that liveth for ever and ever" (Rev. 5:14).

Doubtless there will be things to do and many places to visit during the eternal ages, but of one thing there can be no doubt. When the redeemed church see the nailprints in the hands of the Lord and realize that without His love reaching heaven would have been impossible, they will fall at His feet and worship. Souls who die in faith will live eternally.

DAVID—WHO RESEMBLED
HIS DISTANT COUSIN, PETER

What time I am afraid, I will trust in thee (Ps. 56:3).

In the year 1799 when the armies of Napoleon were sweeping across Europe, his general, Massena, suddenly appeared with 18,000 men on the heights above Feldkirk on the Austrian border. It was Easter Sunday morning, and as the rays of the rising sun shone on the banners and shields of the soldiers, the town council met in an emergency session to decide what action should be taken. Should they send a deputation seeking peace terms with the enemy or defend their town? The aged Dean of the church stood up to remind his parishioners that it was Easter morning, and they were commemorating the resurrection of the Savior. He advised that they should proceed with their celebration. He said, "Let us ring the bells and trust God." The council accepted his advice, and soon the bells of three or four churches were heard all over the countryside. Messena, the French general, listened and came to the conclusion that during the night the Austrian army had arrived to defend the town. He gave orders to break camp and prepare to leave. The town was preserved, and the worshipers had special reasons to remember that glorious Easter deliverance.

The story introduces a text. David said, "What time I am afraid, I will trust in thee." The psalmist offers advice to everyone. There are occasions when even the strongest people tremble and become afraid. Sickness, pain, and the fear of impending surgery bring to our minds all kinds of questions and dread. Financial difficulties and desperation sometimes bring increasing distress. Unsympathetic partners and domestic strife increase tension in homes and offices. Then it becomes easy to doubt, and fear of the future can oppress even the most faithful of God's children. Fear is the enemy of faith, and sometimes our spiritual eyesight grows dim. David said, "When I am afraid, I will trust in Thee." That text is even more attractive when seen in its biblical setting.

First Samuel 21 describes a most dramatic scene when David's life was threatened. Surrounded by enemies and fearing imminent decease, he pretended to be insane, and the spectacle that followed was amazing. The Philistines were watching, and if the king of Gath granted their request, they would have slain the man they did not trust. David saw the animosity in their eyes and desperately wondered what could be done. Suddenly his entire appearance changed as he assumed the role of a maniac. His fingers became as the claws of a great eagle frenziedly trying to climb the city gate. His spittle and saliva trickled down upon his beard, and wild behavior suggested he was a man controlled by demons. The watching king instinctively moved away as David produced a most astonishing display of make-believe. He appeared to be a soul in eternal torment, and the audience became uneasy; they feared the demons might attack them. They believed that every form of mental illness was caused by evil spirits. David was not an actor, and his performance that day bordered on the miraculous. He had been a fugitive running from Saul and finally, fearing for his life, had taken his small company of soldiers to the city of Gath to ask for protection. His desire was granted, but the Philistine lords did not trust the newcomer. They said, "Is not this David, the king of the land? Did they not sing one to another of him, in songs and in dances, saying, Saul hath slain his thousands and David his ten thousands?"

When David perceived his enemies were determined to kill him, "he changed his behavior before them, and feigned himself mad in their hands, and scrabbled on the doors of the gate, and let his spittle fall down upon his beard" (1 Sam. 21:13). Horrified, the king watched the spectacle and, believing David was possessed by demons, expelled him from the country, "And David came to the cave of Adullum." Within the stillness of the mountain sanctuary, David reminisced and, writing Psalm 56:11, said: "In God have I put my trust: I will not be afraid what man can do unto me." Then certain facts became obvious.

David's Difficulties Did Not Mean God had Forsaken Him

The unrehearsed performance of playing the role of a madman was amazing, for the fugitive was not a professional actor. There is evidence that God imparted that ability to David in order to fulfill His own purposes. Even clever men would have needed training to provide such an exhibition. When adverse circumstances threaten the serenity of a Christian, it should never be assumed God has forsaken His child. God moves in mysterious ways His wonders to perform.

76

David's Distress Had Driven Him to Seek Help Outside of the Will of God

Solomon said: "The fear of man bringeth a snare: but whoso putteth his trust in the LORD shall be safe" (Prov. 29:25). He was probably taught this truth by his father. David temporarily forsook the prophets, lost sight of the mighty power of Jehovah, and relying upon himself, sought assistance from a pagan monarch. Such actions could not be pleasing to the Almighty. Believers should abide in God's country where access to the divine presence is always possible. That fact has never changed. The Lord permitted the difficulties to overwhelm His servant because He was trying to bring a wanderer home. Fear and faith cannot live together; one will kill the other.

The Darkest Hour Precedes the Dawn

This was true in the life of David. The darker the night, the more easily are stars seen. When everything goes wrong with Christians, they should look beyond the gloom and ask what God is suggesting. It is important to remember that the Lord not only delivered David from the danger in Gath; He continued to bless His servant and, ultimately, set him upon the throne of Israel. When God has a purpose for His children, He will complete what He has commenced. David and Simon Peter shared similar experiences.

The New Testament describes how the fisherman from Galilee was often overwhelmed by fear and shame. Yet, in his darkest hours, the Light of the World shone into Peter's soul.

Peter Sinking

And in the fourth watch of the night, Jesus went unto them, walking on the sea. And when the disciples saw him walking on the sea, they were troubled, saying, It is a spirit; and they cried out for fear. But straightway Jesus spake unto them, saying, Be of good cheer; It is I; be not afraid. And Peter answered him and said, Lord, if it be thou, bid me come unto thee on the water. And he said, Come. And when Peter was come down out of the ship, he walked on the water, to go to Jesus. But when he saw the wind boisterous, he was afraid; and beginning to sink, he cried, saying, Lord save me. And immediately Jesus stretched forth his hand and caught him, and said unto him, O thou of little faith, wherefore didst thou doubt? (Matt. 14:25–31).

When Simon Peter ceased looking at Jesus, he began to sink. Yet, to his credit it must be remembered that for a while, at least, he did walk on the water. The poet offered great advice when he said, "Never lose sight of Jesus."

Peter Slipping

Then took they him, and led him, and brought him into the high priest's house. And Peter followed afar off. And when they had kindled a fire in the midst of the hall, and were set down together, Peter sat down among them. But a certain maid beheld him as he sat by the fire, and earnestly looked upon him, and said, This man was also with him. And he denied him, saying, Woman, I know him not (Luke 22:54–57).

Poor Simon! He, like David, had also ceased looking at the Lord and was swiftly becoming afraid. He who had been so boastful and self-confident was trembling. Peter should have avoided that fire; it belonged to the enemies of the Savior. He was destined to remember that awful experience throughout the rest of his life. Three times he denied the Lord, and then the sound of a cock crowing brought him face-to-face with reality. Instinctively he turned toward Jesus.

And the Lord turned, and looked upon Peter. And Peter remembered the word of the Lord, how he had said unto him, Before the cock crow, thou shalt deny me thrice. And Peter went out, and wept bitterly (Luke 22:61–62).

Simon did not fall in a moment; he slipped gradually until finally his soul seemed to be plunging into oblivion.

Peter Shamed

And entering into the sepulchre, they saw a young man sitting on the right side, clothed in a long white garment; and they were afraid. And he saith unto them, Be not afraid: Ye seek Jesus of Nazareth, which was crucified: He is risen; he is not

here: behold the place where they laid him. But go your way;
tell his disciples *and Peter* that he goeth before you into Galilee: there shall ye see him, as he said unto you (Mark 16:5–7).

It was significant that after the risen Christ had appeared unto
the Emmaus travelers, they returned to share their good news
with the brethren in Jerusalem. "And they rose up the same hour,
and returned to Jerusalem, and found the eleven gathered together, and them that were with them, saying, The Lord is risen
indeed, and hath appeared to Simon" (Luke 24:33–34). It was
significant that special mention was made of Simon. The disciple surely received that invitation, but apparently had no intention of going anywhere to meet Christ. He was so ashamed of
his conduct at the fire, he could not meet the Lord again. Therefore it became necessary for the Good Shepherd to go in search
of His lost sheep. What happened at that meeting, and what was
said by the Savior remains a mystery. Yet it is evident that the
healing touch of Christ cured Peter's ills and restored the fisherman to newness of life. As David was elevated to the throne of
Israel, so Simon Peter became God's chosen servant on the day
of Pentecost. The apostle, who had been afraid of his enemies,
later wrote: "If ye suffer for righteousness' sake, happy are ye:
and *be not afraid of their terror, neither be troubled*; but sancti-
fy the Lord God in your hearts" (1 Peter 3:14–15).

A delightful story has come from Canada where a very despondent minister received help from a story published in a local newspaper. The local parks committee had been ordered to remove a
line of trees from a certain street that needed widening. As the
workmen were about to begin, the foreman noticed a bird had
built its nest in one of the condemned trees. Seeing that the mother
bird was sitting on the nest, the foreman ordered his men to leave
that particular tree until later. When they returned, they found the
nest filled with wide-mouthed baby robins. Once again they post-
poned felling the tree, and the mother robin was able to tend her
family. Later, the foreman discovered the babies had flown; the
nest was empty. When he removed the nest, he saw something
white woven into the nest. Carefully wiping away the dirt, he
discovered the white object was a part of a small card from a
Sunday School. Printed on it were the words: "We trust in the
Lord our God." That story was printed in a newspaper, and a very

discouraged clergyman believed it to be a message sent by God specially for him. If God could protect the nest of a small Canadian robin, He would surely care for his child. Civilia D. Martin was correct when she wrote:

> Be not dismayed whate'er betide,
> God will take care of you;
> Beneath His wings of love abide,
> God will take care of you.

*Because he hath set his love upon me, therefore will I deliver
him: I will set him on high, because he hath known my name.
He shall call upon me and I will answer him: I will be with him
in trouble; I will deliver him, and honour him. With long life
will I satisfy him, and shew him my salvation (Ps. 91:14–16).*

Seeking for hidden treasure has fascinated men for many centuries. When banks were unknown, people buried their valuables
in the earth. The Savior knew this and said: "The kingdom of
heaven is like unto treasure hid in a field; the which when a man
hath found, he hideth, and for joy thereof goeth and selleth all
that he hath, and buyeth that field" (Matt. 13:44). Today, the
media often supplies news of explorers who dive to the depths of
oceans in the hope of finding ancient ships which sank either in
battle or in storms. They hope to discover artifacts, and great
sums of money are spent on expeditions which often produce
nothing.

It is surprising that the greatest of all possibilities has no
attraction for most of earth's residents. God's treasure is fabu-
lous, but men need a special key to acquire it. David made a list
of things above the price of rubies, and the secret of his success
was described in a single sentence. *"Because he hath set his love
upon me,"* therefore will I do certain things for him.

God appreciates faithful service, and thankfully receives gifts
from those involved in the extension of His kingdom. Yet, above
all gifts, *God loves to be loved.* Many people take all and give
nothing in return, and that has been evident throughout the ages.
The Lord gives to people who forget to return thanks. Jesus saw
this affection when a widow placed two mites into the Temple
offertory. He said it surpassed all the lavish offerings brought by
wealthy Pharisees. When He evaluated the wealthy church in
Laodicea, He said: "I will spue thee out of my mouth" (Rev.
3:16). Love is not superficial and changeable. It is eternal, born
of God. David believed it to be a key capable of opening God's
treasure chest. It could bring to its owner incalculable riches.
The psalmist mentioned various jewels awaiting discovery.

The God Who Saves ... *"Because he hath set his love upon me, therefore will I deliver him"* (v. 14)

David's life was filled with occasions when his existence was threatened, and any one of these could have proved God delighted to deliver His people. Faith is a great asset, but basically it refers to the intellect. Love fills and thrills the soul; it is the cause for gratitude and the reason for sacrificial service. A sound mind with a cold heart is a polished automobile without an engine, a perfect body without life. The Ephesian church was famous for its theology, but condemned because its initial love had disappeared. The leaders of the assembly could deliver excellent speeches about a theme of which they knew little. David knew that to love God passionately was better than all the sacrifices offered in the tabernacle at Shiloh. If a modern combination lock had been on God's treasure chest, love would have been the first digit in the magic number. It cannot be emphasized too much that *God loves to be loved*. His great affection can lift man from the deepest depths of degradation and raise him to unprecedented heights of ecstasy and fellowship. The Creator of the world was famous for His power; Our heavenly Father is known for the love that made salvation possible. The poet was correct when he wrote:

> Amazing love! how can it be
> That Thou, my God, should'st die for me!

The God Who Selects ... *"Because he hath set his love upon me, ... I will set him on high"* (v. 14)

David never forgot he had been a shepherd boy. When Samuel first visited the home of Jesse, the lad had been absent and not considered worthy of being interviewed by the prophet. The ancient record says:

And Samuel said unto Jesse, Are here all thy children? And he said, There remaineth yet the youngest, and, behold, he keepeth the sheep. And Samuel said unto Jesse, Send and fetch him: for we will not sit down till he come hither. And he sent, and brought him in. Now he was ruddy, and withal of a beautiful countenance, and goodly to look to. And the Lord said, Arise, anoint him: for this is he (1 Sam. 16:11–12).

82

After many years David reminisced and considered how the Almighty had lifted him from obscurity to be the ruler of Israel. With the simplicity of a child David had opened his soul to God, and that love enabled him to defeat the approaching giant. It is unfortunate that many people fail to understand the best way to fame is to bow before the Lord. When God said, "I will set him on high," He meant what He promised.

The God Who Speaks . . . *"Because he hath set his love upon me, . . . He shall call upon me, and I will answer him"* (v. 15)

To love God does not provide immunity from trouble. David had more than his share of problems. Sometimes he contributed to his own sorrow, and strife within his family accentuated his pain. God did not prevent storms from reaching His servant; He preferred to be with David in them. It was better to be in danger *with* God than to be elsewhere without Him. The disciples of Jesus learned more when their boat was sinking on the Sea of Galilee than they did on the shore. If Daniel had not been cast into the den of lions, he would not have witnessed God's power over ravenous beasts (see Dan. 6:16). It was only when the Hebrew boys were thrown into the furnace that they discovered one "like the Son of God" awaiting their arrival (see Dan. 3:25). Wisdom is always evident in the way the Lord deals with His children. A mother asked her husband why he persisted in taking his small child into a darkened basement. He replied: "I like to feel her clinging to my hand." It should be remembered that God is our heavenly Father, and "No good thing will He withhold from them that walk uprightly" (Ps. 84:11).

The God Who Sustains . . . *"Because he hath set his love upon me, . . . I will be with him in trouble"* (v. 15)

It is a thrilling experience to listen to the voice of God when one feels abandoned. The disciples of Christ were reassured when they heard their Master rebuking the storm and amazed when the sea became calm. On the other hand, Job was overwhelmed by the worst kind of tempest. It seemed that God had abandoned him when he said: "Oh, that I knew where I might find him! that I might come even to his seat!" (Job 23:3). The Lord was with Job every moment of each day. True faith sees in the dark; it is the "substance of things hoped for, the evidence of things not seen" (Heb. 11:1).

83

Perhaps in some measure Job possessed faith, for, although he appeared to be alone, his love for the Lord never diminished. His loyalty was evident even when he failed to understand why affliction overwhelmed his soul. The angels may have smiled when the suffering man exclaimed: "Though he slay me, yet will I trust in him. . . . He also shall be my salvation" (Job 13:15–16).

The God Who Satisfies . . . *"Because he hath set his love upon me, . . . with long life will I satisfy him"* (v. 16)

Life is a precious jewel. Unless a man suffers excruciating pain or is devastated by shame, he desires to live. Some emotional people make speeches announcing their desire to go to heaven, yet the moment they become ill, they seek a doctor. If their testimony were sincere, they would endeavor to die gracefully! Healthy people who state they are tired of living are unstable, emotional, and unworthy of trust.

There are all kinds of reasons why Christians should continue to live. No souls will be won for Christ after death. That opportunity is for NOW. No crown will be won beyond the grave. That also is for NOW. The longer a man lives, the greater his opportunity of serving Christ. When I first went to South Africa, I was introduced to Daddy Rowlands who met every incoming and outgoing missionary. He could arrange a meeting at any time of the day or night. His service for the Savior was phenomenal. I was so impressed that I said, "He will live a long time, for the Lord would have difficulty finding his replacement." That amazing man lived to be over one hundred years of age, but his glorious example will never die. He was another of whom the Lord said: "With long life will I satisfy him." If you want to reach old age, work hard for Christ!

The God Who Shews . . . *"Because he hath set his love upon me, . . . [I will] shew him my salvation"* (v. 16)

Salvation is the most wonderful of all God's treasures. The divine command created planets, stars, and the precious metals for which men have lived and died. Salvation God did not create. He could only plan to make a dream become a reality. Heaven's wealth could not buy it, and time could not contain it. To lift a sinner from the depths of degradation, to cleanse and clothe him with righteousness, to build a mansion in which he would live

84

eternally was something which redemption alone could accomplish. It involved the death of heaven's Prince, the cooperation of the Almighty, and a ministry to replace ruin with resplendence. It was to be God's finest accomplishment, a task that made Creation seem commonplace.

Man in his wildest dreams could never imagine it nor deserve it. Something conceived in the mind of God would be given to the most unworthy recipients. When the Lord made the world, He saw it was good; when He planned the redemption of sinners, He saw it was better; when the saints are clothed in white raiment, He will know that this will be His greatest achievement.

God promised to reveal this to people who set their love upon Him. It is now evident He has done so. Christ came to make salvation possible; inspired men wrote what was known about Him; and now through the miracle of grace, millions of people can say:

> My Jesus, I love Thee, I know Thou art mine—
> For Thee all the follies of sin I resign;
> My gracious Redeemer, my Savior art Thou:
> If ever I loved Thee, my Jesus, 'tis now.

God honored His promise; He kept His word.

He brought them forth also with silver and gold: and there was not one feeble person among their tribes (Ps. 105:37).

When the government of the United States authorized the effort to deliver Kuwait from the dominance of the aggressor, lavish support was supplied to the American liberators. Millions of gallons of bottled drinking water were sent to alleviate the thirst of the army. Fully equipped hospital ships were ready to receive sick and wounded men, and in a multitude of ways the War Department arranged for every emergency. If the entire population of a great city had, for any reason, to migrate to a new location, similar preparations would be made. Every detail relating to health, comfort, and safety would be considered, and the mass migration would command the attention of the world's media.

It is strange to discover that when two million Hebrews began their journey from Egypt to Canaan, none of these preparations were made. There were no ambulances to carry infirm people, no preparation regarding food nor drink; the people had no weapons to withstand attacks. There were no sick people, and only babies needed attention. It was the only time in history when an entire nation had a clean bill of health. "There was not a feeble person among their tribes" (Ps. 105:37). *The Berkeley Version* of the Scriptures translates the text: "There was not an invalid among their tribes." Spurgeon, the great British preacher, wrote: "And there was not one feeble person among the tribes—a great marvel indeed. The number of their army was very great and yet there was not one in hospital, not one carried in an ambulance, nor limping in the rear. Poverty and oppression had not enfeebled them. Jehovah Raphi had healed them. They carried none of the diseases of Egypt, and felt none of the exhaustion which sore bondage produces. When God calls His people to a long journey, He fits them for it. In the pilgrimage of life, our strength shall be equal to our days. See the contrast between Egypt and Israel—in Egypt one dead in every house, and among the Israelites, not one, so much as limping."[1]

A Continuing Satisfaction . . . *No Joy Is Complete Without God*

Happiness is the music of the soul. The psalmist wrote: "And he brought forth his people with joy, and his chosen with gladness" (Ps. 105:43). "When the LORD turned again the captivity of Zion, we were like them that dream. Then was our mouth filled with laughter, and our tongue with singing; then said they among the heathen, The LORD hath done great things for them. The LORD hath done great things for us; whereof we are glad" (Ps. 126:1–3). When the beggar who sat at the temple gate was healed by Peter and John, it was said: "And he leaping up stood, and walked, and entered with them into the temple, walking, and leaping, and praising God" (Acts 3:8). David was exultant when he said: "I waited patiently for the LORD; and he inclined unto me, and heard my cry. He brought me up also out of an horrible pit, out of the miry clay, and set my feet upon a rock, and established my goings. And he hath put a new song in my mouth, even praise unto our God. Many shall see it, and fear, and shall trust in the LORD" (Ps. 40:1–3).

True happiness depends upon fellowship with God. When Israel forsook the Lord, rejected His messengers, and became the slaves of the Babylonians, songs were not heard in their camps. The psalmist said: "By the rivers of Babylon, there we sat down, yea, we wept, when we remembered Zion. We hanged our harps upon the willows in the midst thereof. For there they that carried us away captive required of us a song; and they that wasted us required of us mirth, saying, Sing us one of the songs of Zion. How shall we sing the LORD's song in a strange land?" (Ps. 137:1–4). It is difficult to produce inspired music when the Divine Composer is excluded from the human heart.

A Constant Supply . . . *No Provision Is Sufficient Without God*

And the Egyptians were urgent upon the people, that they might send them out of the land in haste; for they said, We be all dead men. And the people took their dough before it was leavened, their kneadingtroughs being bound up in their clothes upon their shoulders. . . . And a mixed multitude went up also with them; and flocks, and herds, even very much cattle. And they baked unleavened cakes of the dough which they brought forth out of Egypt, for it was not leavened; because they were thrust out of Egypt, and could not tarry; neither had they prepared for themselves any victual (Exod. 12:33–39).

87

When the children of Israel made a hurried departure from Egypt, they had little time to prepare for their journey. Such animals as they possessed were quickly rounded up, and the mass migration commenced. Probably most of the cattle belonged to the mixed multitude that decided to accompany the Hebrews. These herds provided food for the travelers during the initial stages of their long journey. Unfortunately, those supplies soon diminished, for the large company consumed a great amount of food. It was impossible for more than two million people to live off the land, and unless God had rained manna from heaven, the people would have died in the wilderness.

The fact that God is able to provide what His people need is a lesson which all nations should learn. Misers may amass a great fortune but finally discover wealth can only pay for a funeral. Athletes may become immensely popular, but age undermines their skill, and younger people claim their fame. Kings, queens, and other rulers of nations may appear to be irreplaceable, but death terminates their activities. Immortality is unobtainable unless God holds out His hand. Sometimes the Lord performs miracles to accomplish His purposes, but at other times He uses different methods to assist His children. He sent manna to feed the children of Israel, but He also supplied quails (Exod. 16:13). Werner Keller says: "The Exodus of the Israelites began in the spring; the time of the great bird migrations. From Africa, which in summer becomes unbearably hot and dry, the birds have, from time immemorial, migrated to Europe along two routes. One goes via the west coast of Africa to Spain; the other via the eastern Mediterranean to the Balkans. In the early months of the year, quails together with other birds, fly across the Red Sea, which they must cross on the eastern route. Exhausted by their long flight, they alight on its flat shores to gather fresh strength for the next stage of their journey over the high mountains to the Mediterranean. Even today the Bedouins of this area catch the exhausted birds in spring and autumn by hand."[2]

A Ceaseless Safety . . . *No Strength Is Enough Without God*

And the LORD went before them by day in a pillar of a cloud, to lead them the way; and by night in a pillar of fire, to give them light; to go by day and night: He took not away the pillar of the cloud by day, nor the pillar of fire by night, from before the people (Exod. 13:21–22).

88

The Bible says there were "about six hundred thousand on foot that were men, beside children" (Exod. 12:37). Apparently the people only possessed homemade spears and lances; they had no chariots of iron, for these would have been confiscated by Pharaoh. Probably many of the men were blacksmiths who were skilled in working with iron. Within a short period of time some of Israel's males would have been able to defend against aggression, and ultimately Israel possessed a great army. A pillar of cloud led them by day, and a pillar of fire by night. They never marched too far from wells and oases, and occasionally it was necessary to travel at night to escape the relentless heat of the day. Few enemies existed in the uninhabited wilderness, but as history reveals, the greatest danger came from within the camp.

When people begin to criticize God, even empires can disintegrate. If the Lord is excluded from the counsel of men, even the strongest weapons of war may become useless. If God withdraws support, human effort becomes inadequate. The prophet, Zechariah, expressed this fact when he wrote: "Not by might, nor by power, but by my spirit, saith the LORD" (Zech. 4:6).

A Complete Security . . . *No Future Is Safe Without God*

> This book of the Law shall not depart out of thy mouth; but thou shalt meditate therein day and night, that thou mayest observe to do according to all that is written therein: for then thou shalt make thy way prosperous, and then thou shalt have good success. Have not I commanded thee? Be strong and of a good courage; be not afraid, neither be thou dismayed: for the Lord thy God is with thee withersoever thou goest (Josh. 1:8–9).

It was over; the wilderness ordeal had terminated. Innumerable graves were all through the wilderness, for two million people had died, and a complete generation, with the exception of two men, had perished. Moses had climbed the mountain of God but had not returned. Somewhere in the solitude God had gently laid His servant to rest. Joshua had become the new leader of Israel, but the future was ominous as, once again, the nation stood at the crossroads of destiny. Forty years earlier the Hebrews had refused to enter Canaan, and had consequently wandered aimlessly through the wilderness. Now they were to enter the land where enemies were giants. The entire responsibility of leadership rested upon the shoulders of Joshua. Perhaps he was apprehensive; his task was frightening. How could he with an army of untrained men overcome the Canaanites who made the Hebrews feel like grasshoppers (see Num. 13:33)? Three simple facts explain his success.

An Unfailing God . . . *The Command to Serve*

God's promise was reassuring. "There shall not any man be able to stand before thee all the days of thy life: As I was with Moses, so I will be with thee: I will not fail thee, nor forsake thee" (Josh. 1:5). The new leader had enjoyed fellowship with the departed Moses. He was now assured the faithfulness of God would remain unchanged.

The Unwavering Guide . . . *A Challenge to Succeed*

Throughout the journey in the wilderness the guidance of God had been unmistakable. By day and night the pillars of the cloud and fire had led the nomads. Now Joshua was assured God's presence would remain. The Lord had said: "But the land whither ye go to possess it, is a land of hills and valleys, and drinketh water of the rain of heaven" (Deut. 11:11). Life has always been filled with high and low experiences, but God promised to give rain in both areas. Obedient people could not wander beyond the reach of His care.

An Unseen General . . . *A Companion to Share*

It must have been a thrilling experience to follow the cloud by day and the fire by night, but that joy was to be surpassed.

And it came to pass, when Joshua was by Jericho, that he lifted up his eyes, and looked, and, behold, there stood a man over against him with his sword drawn in his hand: and Joshua went unto him, and said unto him, Art thou for us or for our adversaries? And he said, Nay; but as captain of the host of the LORD am I now come. And Joshua fell on his face to the earth, and did worship, and said unto him, What saith my lord unto his servant? And the captain of the LORD's host said unto Joshua, Loose thy shoe from off thy foot; for the place whereon thou standest is holy. And Joshua did so (Josh. 5:13–15).

The clouds above the tabernacle were symbols of the divine presence; the captain of the host was the Lord himself. Unseen, but always present, He guaranteed that Joshua would never be alone. The leader of Israel would have appreciated the words of Daniel W. Whittle (1840–1903):

Never a trial that He is not there,
Never a burden that He doth not bear,
Never a sorrow that He doth not share,
Moment by moment, I'm under His care.

Moment by moment I'm kept in His love;
Moment by moment I've life from above;
Looking to Jesus till glory doth shine;
Moment by moment, O Lord, I am thine.

1. Charles Spurgeon, *Great Verses from the Psalms* (Grand Rapids: Zondervan Publishing House, 1977), 204–5.
2. Werner Keller, *The Bible as History* (New York: William Morrow and Company, 1956), 120.

Is there no balm in Gilead; is there no physician there? why then is not the health of the daughter of my people recovered? (Jer. 8:22).

Gilead was famous for trees that produced medicinal balm. It is believed the Queen of Sheba brought seeds to Solomon, and her gift led to a lucrative industry. The scraggy trees had few leaves but produced small white flowers. When the trunk was pierced, it exuded a sticky substance that quickly hardened into globules that were easily removed from the bark. This was used in the manufacture of medicine upon which physicians relied when treating their patients. Gilead had many doctors whose fame spread throughout the country. The prophet's references to these physicians provide food for thought.

A Sad Predicament . . . *Prevailing*

Jeremiah, the prophet of God, was worried; the anxiety in his soul indicated fear of the future. He remembered how the Lord had said: "There shall be no grapes on the vine, nor figs on the fig tree, and the leaf shall fade; and the things that I have given them shall pass away from them" (Jer. 8:13). He said: "We looked for peace, but no good came; and for a time of health, and behold trouble!" (Jer. 8:15). Israel had become a derelict nation, and the ominous words of the Almighty were clouds obliterating the sunshine. "Be astonished, O ye heavens, at this, and be horribly afraid, be ye very desolate, saith the LORD. For my people have committed two evils; they have forsaken me the fountain of living waters, and hewed them out cisterns, broken cisterns, that can hold no water. Is Israel a servant? is he a houseborn slave? why is he spoiled?" (Jer. 2:12–14). "But where are the gods that thou hast made thee? Let them arise, if they can save thee in the time of thy trouble: for according to the number of thy cities are thy gods, O Judah" (Jer. 2:28).

It was unbelievable that the kingdom that had reached unprecedented heights of excellence during the reign of Solomon had degenerated to the level of slavery. The tribes that had proclaimed the magnificence of Jehovah had erected idols

92

throughout their cities. Such degradation was inexcusable, and the sorrowful prophet could not blame God for the catastrophes that had fallen upon the nation. Captivity was inevitable, and hunger was already spreading through the land. Prolonged drought had ruined the crops, but the unrepentant people continued to make idols and were following a course of self-destruction. Jeremiah stood in the midst of the people and asked: "Is there no balm in Gilead; is there no physician there? Why then is not the health of the daughter of my people recovered?"

There might have been two reasons for his questions. Since the balm of Gilead was considered to be a gift from heaven, the people could have refused to avail themselves of the God-given remedy. If the precious substance had failed to cure the ailments of the people, the sufferers had refused to appeal to the giver of every good and perfect gift. Their attitude resembled that of a later generation which said, "We have no king but Caesar." Today's world reflects the events that took place in Israel. It is not difficult to believe that all nations are approaching economic and spiritual disaster. Crime is increasing, prisons are overcrowded, gangs of irresponsible youths terrorize communities, and, for the most part, governments and citizens remain helpless. Unfortunately, many of the churches are ineffective. People prefer to worship the gods of sport, worldly attractions, and sex. Preachers who recommend a return to the "Old Time Religion" are considered relics of a bygone age. The people of the twentieth century ignore the Great Physician in order to patronize their own doctors.

A Stupid Potentate . . . *Procrastinating*

And Asa in the thirty and ninth year of his reign was diseased in his feet, until his disease was exceeding great: yet in his disease he sought not to the Lord, but to the physicians. And Asa slept with his fathers, and died in the one and fortieth year of his reign (2 Chron. 16:12–13).

Asa the king of Judah became a pathetic monarch. There may be an excuse for a man who never knew God, but when a person has known fellowship with the Almighty and then permits pride to destroy the relationship, he exhibits inexcusable folly. The story of this disappointing monarch may be considered under six headings. His faith, fame, foolishness, fate, fear, and funeral.

His Faith

Asa belonged to a very large family; his father Abijah had fourteen wives, twenty-two sons, and sixteen daughters (2 Chron. 13:21). He was a mighty warrior who valued military conquests more than moral and spiritual fidelity. When he succeeded to the throne he inherited a kingdom filled with idols, high places, images, and groves where idolatry was unashamedly practiced (2 Chron. 14:1–3). The reforms instituted by the incoming king were sensational, and Asa's actions became international news. It was said prior to his coronation: "Now for a long season Israel hath been without the true God, and without a teaching priest, and without law" (2 Chron. 15:3). Asa became known for his obedience to the laws of Jehovah.

His Fame

Asa's onslaught upon the enemies of Jehovah was almost unprecedented, and his foes hesitated before attacking the Hebrews. The Jews were prosperous, and revival came to Israel. The Lord was demonstrating the reliability of a promise made by Jesus centuries later. "But seek ye first the kingdom of God, and his righteousness; and all these things shall be added unto you" (Matt. 6:33).

His Foolishness

"In the six and thirtieth year of the reign of Asa Baasha the king of Israel came up against Judah. . . . Then Asa brought out silver and gold out of the treasures of the house of the LORD and of the king's house, and sent to Ben-hadad king of Syria, that dwelt at Damascus, saying, There is a league between me and thee, as there was between my father and thy father: Behold, I have sent thee silver and gold; go, break thy league with Baasha king of Israel, that he may depart from me" (2 Chron. 16:1–3). Asa's suggestion revealed he had more trust in a heathen neighbor than in Jehovah. When the prophet Hanani rebuked the monarch, Asa became enraged and imprisoned the messenger of God.

His Fate

"Then Asa was wroth with the seer, and put him in a prison house; for he was in a rage with him because of this thing. And Asa oppressed some of the people the same time. . . . And Asa in

94

*the thirty and ninth year of his reign was diseased in his feet,
until his disease was exceeding great"* (2 Chron. 16:10–12). Asa
should have been a wiser man, but when pride influences decisions, better judgments are often ignored. The prophet, Azariah,
had warned the monarch saying: "The LORD is with you, while
ye be with him; and if ye seek him he will be found of you; but
if ye forsake him, he will forsake you" (2 Chron. 15:2). When
the counsel of God is forsaken, trouble quickly follows. The
affliction in Asa's feet was caused by malfunctions in his soul.
He who plays with fire is likely to be burned.

His Fear

*"In his disease he sought not to the LORD but to the physicians,
and died in the one and fortieth year of his reign"* (2 Chron.
16:12–13). It is worthy of attention that the king's illness lasted
two years, and during that time, the ailing monarch repeatedly
visited the royal physicians; even the balm of Gilead was ineffective. Throughout that period the pity of the Almighty was
matched only by the pride of Asa. He knew what needed to be
done, but refused to do it.

His Funeral

*"And they buried him in his own sepulchres, which he had
made for himself in the city of David, and laid him in the bed
which was filled with sweet odours and diverse kinds of spices
prepared by the apothecaries' art; and they made a very great
burning for him"* (2 Chron. 16:14). Asa's funeral was one of the
most impressive ever witnessed in Israel. It was interesting that
the king made lavish preparation for the repose of his body, but
neglected the future of his soul. He was given a great farewell by
his subjects, but it is extremely doubtful if he received an equivalent welcome when he stood in the presence of God. Actually,
the unfortunate man died before his time. The great burning of
enormous quantities of spices made the atmosphere heavy with
perfume. Regrettably, the dead king was unable to appreciate the
tribute being paid to him.

A Severe Problem . . . *Persisting*

And a certain woman, which had an issue of blood twelve
years, and had suffered many things of many physicians, and

had spent all that she had, and was nothing bettered, but rather grew worse, when she had heard of Jesus, came in the press behind, and touched his garments (Mark 5:25–27).

The woman was impoverished and desperate. A very distressing hemorrhaging had baffled the physicians whose fees were greater than their skill. She had been treated by numerous doctors, but her disappearing savings had made further visits to the doctors impossible. Rekindling hope had maintained her for twelve years, but, finally, she reached the end of her financial resources. Then one day she heard of another Physician, who never charged for His services. It was difficult to believe the rumors, but friends assured her that the stories were true.

She stood in the crowd and waited; the new doctor was about to visit the home of Jairus, one of the city's most respected citizens. When the woman saw the Savior, her faith deepened, and she whispered, "If I may touch but his clothes, I shall be whole. And straightway the fountain of her blood was dried up; and she felt in her body that she was healed of that plague. . . . And he [Jesus] said unto her, Daughter, thy faith hath made thee whole; go in peace, and be whole of thy plague" (Mark 5:28–29, 34).

It is difficult to avoid the conclusion that if the ancient Hebrews and Asa, the king of Judah, had been as wise, their problems would have been solved, burdens lifted, and their happiness would have been overwhelming. God is always willing to help His children, but He expects cooperation.

> Oh, touch the hem of His garment:
> And thou too, shalt be free,
> His saving power, this very hour,
> Shall give new life to thee.

JEREMIAH—WHO PLACED HIS
MONEY WHERE HIS MOUTH WAS

*And I bought the field of Hanameel my uncle's son, that was
in Anathoth, and weighed him the money, even seventeen
shekels of silver (Jer. 32:9).*

The prophet, Jeremiah, ministered during the most depressing
days of Israel's history. The country was being overrun by
Babylonian soldiers; the crops were ruined, and the land
destroyed. Even Jehovah was annoyed by His obstinate people.
The prophet had been imprisoned within the king's palace; the
destruction of Jerusalem was inevitable; the market value of
everything had reached rock bottom.

Jeremiah had a cousin, the son of Shallum. He was a shrewd
businessman, and an expert at selling useless land. He owned a
field near Anathoth, but realized it would soon be worthless.
According to Hebrew law no property could be sold unless family members first had a chance to purchase it. Jeremiah had a
prior claim on that field, and maybe his cousin had heard of the
strange predictions being made by his relative. He carefully
planned his movements, but was unaware God had warned Jeremiah what was being arranged.

"So Hanameel mine uncle's son came to me in the court of
the prison according to the word of the LORD, and said unto me,
Buy my field, I pray thee, that is in Anathoth, which is in the
country of Benjamin: for the right of inheritance is thine, and the
redemption is thine; buy it for thyself. Then I knew that this was
the word of the LORD. And I bought the field of Hanameel my
uncle's son that was in Anathoth, and weighed him the money,
even seventeen shekels of silver" (Jer. 32:8–9).

A Jew and His Fear . . . *Disturbing*

The laws referring to the sale of Jewish property were very
strict. Sales to foreigners were forbidden, and even when adverse circumstances impoverished the owner, no transaction
could be completed unless the next of kin had been given an
opportunity to make the purchase. Yet, in spite of anything
sold, everything reverted to its original owner at the year of
Jubilee. Evidently the cousin of Jeremiah had either bought or

97

inherited a field near Anathoth, but his shrewd mind warned him it was urgently necessary to get rid of the property; it would soon be without value. The life of Jeremiah revolved around the promises of God. His cousin apparently had no faith in what might be. He lived only for the present and believed God helped those who helped themselves. The fact that he was more or less selling useless land to a member of his family was unimportant. He believed that if Jeremiah made a bad bargain, it was his own fault, for Anathoth would have been wiser not to purchase deteriorated property.

Many years later when the Lord sent a letter to His church at Philadelphia, He said, "Hold that fast which thou hast, that no man take thy crown" (Rev. 3:11). That command should never be forgotten. Even Esau sold his most cherished possession to Jacob because, for the moment, an appetizing meal seemed to be more attractive than gold (see Gen. 25:29–34). Some things are too valuable either to sell or exchange! Esau's stomach ran away with his brain.[1] It is disconcerting to remember that some of God's most promising servants failed in their mission, because they neglected to hold fast that which they already possessed. Whatever Judas might have gained from his being with the Lord was ruined by His desire for money. It was claimed that Solomon was the wisest man in the world, but his wisdom was sacrificed on an altar of lust. It remains a profound mystery why that intelligent ruler should become so foolish. His collapse adds meaning to the words of Paul: "Wherefore let him that thinketh he standeth take heed lest he fall" (1 Cor. 10:12). It appeared that Jeremiah's cousin never considered these facts. He thought only of money and probably died a pauper.

Jeremiah and His Finances . . . *Discerning*

The imprisoned prophet awaited the arrival of his scheming cousin. Perhaps the visitor had heard of the things promised by God to Israel, but whether or not he believed those predictions is a matter of conjecture. Maybe the man saw an opportunity to test the sincerity of his relative. Would the prophet be willing to put his money where his mouth was? If Jeremiah truly believed what he was preaching, he might be tempted to make money by buying and later reselling the land. God had said: "Houses and fields and vineyards shall be possessed again in this land" (Jer.

98

32:15). Hanameel probably congratulated himself on being a very astute businessman.

> "And I bought the field of Hanameel my uncle's son, that was in Anathoth, and weighed him the money, even seventeen shekels of silver. And I subscribed the evidence, and sealed it, and took witnesses, and weighed him the money in the balances. So I took the evidence of the purchase, both that which was sealed according to the law and custom, and that which was open: And I gave the evidence of the purchase unto Baruch . . . in the sight of Hanameel . . . in the presence of witnesses that subscribed the book of the purchase, before all the Jews that sat in the court of the prison. And I charged Baruch before them, saying, Thus saith the LORD of hosts, the God of Israel, Take these evidences, this evidence of the purchase, both which is sealed, and this evidence which is open; and put them in an earthen vessel, that they may continue many days. For thus saith the LORD of hosts, the God of Israel; Houses and fields and vineyards shall be possessed again in this land" (Jer. 32:9–15).

The completion of the legal documents and their being placed in an earthen jar to protect them from dampness suggests that God's servant was fully aware that many years would pass before the fulfillment of his predictions. Jeremiah was completely convinced of the faithfulness of God. He could have used his money to purchase his freedom or to obtain favors to brighten his incarceration. Probably he was not even interested in such amenities. He was God's servant; his future lay in almighty hands.

Jehovah and His Faithfulness . . . *Delivering*

The thoughtfulness of Jeremiah not only guaranteed the safety of his investment, it provided evidence, should people forget or deny the transaction, that the word of the Lord was completely trustworthy. Conditions within Jerusalem were swiftly deteriorating. Advancing armies had cut the supply routes, and increasing hunger was destroying the confidence of the defenders of the city. Jeremiah had been temporarily released from confinement in the hope he would cease being a prophet of doom. He had repeated and even written his predictions of disaster, but the defiant monarch had burned the manuscript (see Jer. 36:22–26). The prophet was instructed by God to write another message using identical words. This angered the noblemen, and their demands for the destruction of the preacher persuaded the king to accede to their requests. "Then Zedekiah the king said, Behold he is in your hand: for the king is not he that can do anything against you. Then took they Jeremiah and cast him into the dungeon . . . that was in the court of the prison: and they let down Jeremiah with cords. And in the dungeon there was no water, but mire: so Jeremiah sunk in the mire" (Jer. 38:5–6).

Poor man! He was sitting in mud at the bottom of the well and had neither food nor water. His outlook was exceedingly bleak. He had every reason in the world to be depressed.

"Now when Ebed-melech the Ethiopian, one of the eunuchs which was in the king's house, heard that they had put Jeremiah in the dungeon; the king then sitting in the gate of Benjamin; Ebed-melech went forth out of the king's house, and spake to the king, saying, My lord the king, these men have done evil in all that they have done to Jeremiah the prophet, whom they have cast into the dungeon; and he is like to die for hunger in the place where he is: for there is no more bread in the city. Then the king commanded Ebed-melech the Ethiopian, saying, Take from hence thirty men with thee, and take up Jeremiah the prophet out of the dungeon, before he die. So Ebed-melech took the men with him, and went into the house of the king under the treasury, and took thence old cast clouts and old rotten rags, and let them down by cords into the dungeon to Jeremiah. And Ebed-melech the Ethiopian said unto Jeremiah, Put now these old cast clouts and old rotten rags under thine armholes under the cords. And Jeremiah did so. So they drew up Jeremiah with cords, and took him up out of the dungeon: and Jeremiah remained in the court of the prison" (Jer. 38:7–13).

Sometimes God uses the most unlikely methods to perform miracles. Ebed-melech was a captive from Africa. His loyalty to the king must have been commendable, for he had access to the king's presence where he interceded for the prophet's release. Gently, carefully, Jeremiah was rescued and bathed. God sent a black man to help Jeremiah, an earthquake to help Paul and Silas, and a fish to help pay the taxes for the Lord and Simon

Peter. Evidently, He has a great variety of servants capable of meeting the needs of His children.

Many years elapsed before Jeremiah's predictions were fulfilled. The returning exiles from Babylon began to plow the land, rebuild the cities, and restore prosperity to the desolate country. Nothing more was said of the documents preserved in the earthen vessel, but the carefulness of Jeremiah in making his arrangements revealed him to be a man competent to fulfill his assignments. He was a gracious servant of Jehovah who cared for the reputation of his Master. He reminds one of an event which occurred during one of Sir Ernest Henry Shackleton's voyages to Antarctica. On one occasion the leader was obliged to leave some of his men on an island, promising to return for them as soon as possible. Unfavorable conditions delayed that return, and it was only on his fourth attempt that Shackleton found a channel through the ice. Passing through that opening as quickly as possible, the explorer was delighted to find his men ready to board his vessel immediately. They escaped before the inlet was closed by ice. The famous explorer asked why his men were ready to embark at a moment's notice and was told: "Our leader rolled up his sleeping bag every morning and said, 'Get your things ready; the boss might come today.'" Jeremiah was a man of that caliber, and all Christians should emulate his example.

1. Ivor Powell, *Bible Cameos* (Grand Rapids: Kregel Publications, 1985), 11–12.

The same hour was the thing fulfilled upon Nebuchadnezzar: and he was driven from men, and did eat grass as oxen, and his body was wet with the dew of heaven, till his hairs were grown like eagles' feathers, and his nails like birds' claws (Dan. 4:33).

The Lord has always been engaged in the work of reclaiming men and women. Sometimes He failed as with Judas; with others He succeeded as He did with Saul of Tarsus. His life-changing efforts have been continued by rescue missions around the world, and it is informative to know that Jesus said: "Likewise I say unto you, there is joy in the presence of the angels of God over one sinner that repenteth" (Luke 15:10). The statement suggests that the heavenly hosts are aware of events taking place on earth and follow with interest every attempt made to redeem sinners. Even in the Old Testament era outstanding conversations were reported. Naaman, the captain of the hosts of Syria, was cleansed of leprosy and afterward said, "Now I know there is no God in all the earth, but in Israel" (2 Kings 5:15). Probably the most sensational convert won for God in those ancient times never received the publicity he deserved. It took a long time for the Lord to change the life of Nebuchadnezzar, but the manner in which this was accomplished may be considered in six stages.

God Witnessing . . . *How Surprising*

The king of Babylon was probably the greatest man in the world. He was a Gentile, and in the estimation of the Hebrews was unclean, for his ruthless legions devastated and defiled their homeland. Had anyone suggested he would become a worshiper of Jehovah, the notion would have been ridiculed. Yet the Lord had a special interest in that ruler and planned to win his allegiance. The story of his conversion makes excellent reading.

Daniel was a Hebrew prophet who lived among the slaves. He possessed a variety of gifts, and consequently his fame spread throughout Babylon. The king first became aware of the young prophet when his own magicians failed to explain a dream. Becoming infuriated with the incompetence of his subjects, he ordered their execution, but Daniel interceded on their behalf and succeeded in explaining the troublesome dream.

The king answered unto Daniel, and said, Of a truth it is, that your God is a God of gods, and a Lord of kings. . . . Then the king made Daniel a great man, and gave him many great gifts . . . (Dan. 2:47–48).

As far as is known, that was the first time God succeeded in capturing the attention of the king of Babylon. Unfortunately his outburst was a spontaneous impulse, and it became necessary for the Lord to renew His efforts. When the three Hebrew boys were cast into the burning, fiery furnace, Nebuchadnezzar was astonished and said, "Lo, I see four men loose, walking in the midst of the fire, and they have no hurt; and the form of the fourth is like the Son of God" (Dan. 3:25).

Once again Nebuchadnezzar recognized the purpose and power of the Almighty, but remained an idolater. He exclaimed, "There is no other God that can deliver after this sort" (Dan. 3:29). It was disappointing when he continued to worship idols and said Daniel's success was made possible by "the spirit of the holy gods" (see Dan. 4:8). He resembled the people of another age who "feared the Lord and served their own gods . . ." (2 Kings 17:33). Nevertheless, God never abandoned His efforts to win the heathen king, and that was truly surprising, for Nebuchadnezzar was a Gentile.

God Warning . . . *How Serious*

The Lord seemed to be following the advice of the old adage, "If at first, you don't succeed, try, try again." Once more, the king sought the meaning of a dream. He had seen a great tree that appeared to reach the heavens. Then, a destroyer cut it down, leaving its roots in the ground. The monarch could not understand why the stump was likened to an insane man who lived among animals. Daniel frowned when he recognized the warning that God was giving to the self-reliant ruler. The great tree was Nebuchadnezzar, who was about to be humiliated and become as a beast.

This is the interpretation, O king, and this is the decree of the most High, which is come upon my lord the king. That they shall drive thee from men, and thy dwelling shall be with the beasts of the field, and they shall make thee to eat grass as

103

oxen, and they shall wet thee with the dew of heaven, and
seven times shall pass over thee, till thou know that the most
High ruleth in the kingdom of men, and giveth it to whomsoever he will (Dan. 4:24–25).

Fear, faith, and foolishness fought for mastery within the king's
soul. He knew there were things to do but did nothing. He had
received a warning from the God of heaven, but whether the
man understood the full significance of the message may be
debatable. He could have avoided a lot of trouble but was very
stupid. When God speaks, wise men listen.

God Waiting . . . *How Suggestive*

At the end of twelve months (Dan. 4:29).

It was truly amazing that God waited for a year before per-
mitting judgment to overwhelm that guilty ruler. Why did He
wait so long? The Lord was waiting for the man to repent of his
sins and accept the word of Daniel. Had these things happened
during the year of grace, Nebuchadnezzar would not have lost
his reason. This was the type of kindness shown to the people of
Noah's generation. They listened to the preacher's warnings, but
ridiculed him. They saw the construction of the ark, the arrival
of the animals, and remained unimpressed. When the ship was
ready to sail, there came a strange delay.

Then went in two and two unto Noah into the ark, the male
and the female, as God had commanded Noah. And it came to
pass after seven days, that the waters of the flood were upon
the earth (Gen. 7:9–10).

Jehovah waited seven days in the hope that people would
respond to the preaching of Noah. An identical opportunity was
given to Nebuchadnezzar. The apostle John sent messages to the
seven churches of Asia, and emphasized that Christ was *standing* outside the door of the assembly in Laodicea. Perhaps the
best way to understand this statement is to ask the question—
how long has He been waiting for other people to respond to His
entreaty?

104

God Watching . . . *How Solemn*

And at the end of the day I Nebuchadnezzar lifted up mine eyes unto heaven, and mine understanding returned unto me, and I blessed the most High, and I praised and honoured him that liveth forever, whose dominion is an everlasting dominion, and his kingdom is from generation to generation (Dan. 4:34).

At this part of the story the restored king gives his own testimony. Evidently he should have prayed twelve months earlier. The distressed monarch believed he had been forsaken by everybody. When his noblemen saw him eating with the cattle, they were astounded. He had lost his self-respect. The nails on his hands and toes had grown to be like the claws of an eagle. His hair had become matted and was as feathers clinging to his head. He was repulsive and obnoxious as he crawled among cattle to eat grass.

Sometimes it is easy to believe God has become indifferent to human need. Elijah exclaimed: "I, even I only, am left; and they seek my life, to take it away" (1 Kings 19:14). David, the fugitive, became despondent and asked: "Why art thou cast down, O my soul? and why art thou disquieted in me?" (Ps. 42:5). When disaster appears to be inevitable, God is never far away. "Like as a father pitieth his children, so the LORD pitieth them that fear him" (Ps. 103:13). Probably, God was never closer to King Nebuchadnezzar than when the man lost his sanity. The prodigal son would have sympathized with the Babylonian, for they both shared the food of animals. The king ate grass; the prodigal stole pigs' food.

God Working . . . *How Splendid*

And at the end of the day I Nebuchadnezzar lifted up mine eyes unto heaven, and mine understanding returned unto me (Dan. 4:34).

Apparently the Lord was watching intently; everything was proceeding according to His plan. It is impossible to probe the depths of a deranged mind, but evidently God was waiting for the man to "lift up his eyes unto heaven." Amid all the terrible fantasies that flooded Nebuchadnezzar's mind, suddenly, for a moment at least, light from the Sun of Righteousness reached his troubled soul, and God heard his whispered prayer. Many years later Jesus of Nazareth could have been considering these facts when He said, "But seek ye first the kingdom of God, and his righteousness; and all these things shall be added unto you" (Matt. 6:33). Constantly, the Lord had been awaiting the moment when He would be able to complete His work. It would be wonderful to restore the king's sanity, but infinitely greater to eradicate idols from his affection.

God Winning . . . *How Sublime*

God does everything possible to help people, but unfortunately there are limits to His capabilities. John described the Savior as standing outside the door of the Laodicean church, knocking and seeking admission. How long did Christ continue knocking? The Savior cannot enjoy fellowship within the soul until He is permitted to enter.

> Mine honour and brightness returned unto me; and my counsellors and my lords sought unto me; and I was established in my kingdom, and excellent majesty was added unto me. Now I Nebuchadnezzar praise and extol and honour the King of heaven, all whose works are truth, and his ways judgment: and those that walk in pride he is able to abase (Dan. 4:36–37).

If the king of Babylon ever became acquainted with the Hebrew Scriptures, one verse would command his attention and capture his affection. The psalmist wrote: "When the LORD turned again the captivity of Zion, we were like them that dream. Then was our mouth filled with laughter, and our tongue with singing: then said they among the heathen, The LORD hath done great things for them. The LORD hath done great things for *us*; whereof we are glad" (Ps. 126:1–3). The redemption of that ancient monarch is one of the most thrilling accounts in the Bible: it is a monument to the grace of God that continually seeks the souls of lost men.

The king of Babylon would have appreciated the words of Dr. George Matheson:

> O Love that wilt not let me go,
> I rest my weary soul in Thee;
> I give Thee back the life I owe,
> That in Thine ocean depths its flow
> May richer, fuller be.

106

And he that earneth wages earneth wages to put it into a bag with holes (Hag. 1:6).

Haggai was a prophet who ministered to people who returned from Babylon. The early enthusiasm which was evident under the leadership of Ezra and Nehemiah had waned; the nation had become decadent. They abandoned the repair of the temple and gave attention to the erection of their homes. They said, "There is plenty of time to build the sanctuary; we must first attend to our needs." Their attitude displeased God and the prophet. Apathy was always the enemy of enthusiasm. Haggai watched as they worked ceaselessly to earn money and said, "You are putting your money into a bag filled with holes—working hard and getting nowhere!"[1]

The prophet bequeathed to posterity a text worthy of consideration. Much more than money may fall through holes in our pockets! I remember staying in an Australian home where the host was continually losing cash. He had a hole in his pants, and as fast as he put money into his pocket, it dropped to the floor. He appeared unimpressed when, day after day, I returned what I had found. It is not difficult to discover in the Scriptures people who had holes in their pockets. Treasures lost in this manner may never return. It is better to repair the pocket than to suffer immeasurable loss.

The Pocket of Affection

The church at Ephesus was among the greatest New Testament assemblies. The work done there by Paul had returned excellent dividends, for in every aspect of Christian endeavor, the members excelled.

Unto the angel of the church at Ephesus write; These things saith he that holdeth the seven stars in his right hand, who walketh in the midst of the seven golden candlesticks; I know thy works, and thy labour, and thy patience, and how thou canst not bear them which are evil: and thou hast tried them which say they are apostles, and are not, and hast found them liars: And hast borne, and hast patience, and for my name's sake hast laboured, and hast not fainted (Rev. 2:1–3).

107

During persecution the members had been patient and through difficulties, persistent. When false teaching threatened to undermine the faith, courageously they had obeyed the truth preached by Paul. The meetings were filled with devoted worshipers, and apparently they were all that could be desired. It was surprising and unexpected when the Savior said they had left their first love. The labor for Christ had been spoiled by a hole in their pocket of affection.

When a person falls in love for the first time, a special combination of devotion, admiration, and enthusiasm produces ecstasy that exhilarates the soul and transforms behavior. That initial love increases the determination to please, but unfortunately, it often disappears quickly. Even Christians may allow increasing labor to decrease their time for a closer relationship with Christ. To work hard for the Lord is very essential, but unless the labor is inspired by a glowing heart, service can become mechanical and ineffective.

The Pocket of Attraction

And it came to pass in an eveningtide, that David arose from off his bed, and walked upon the roof of the king's house: and from the roof he saw a woman washing herself; and the woman was very beautiful to look upon (2 Sam. 11:2).

David was a man of moods. He reached heights of devotion and depths of defeat and failure. He exultantly cried, "One thing have I desired of the LORD, that will I seek after; that I may dwell in the house of the LORD all the days of my life, to behold the beauty of the LORD, and to inquire in his temple" (Ps. 27:4). At another time he lusted after a beautiful woman, murdered her husband, and in bitter remorse said, "Have mercy upon me, O God, according to thy lovingkindness: according unto the multitude of thy tender mercies blot out my transgressions. Wash me thoroughly from mine iniquity, and cleanse me from my sin. For I acknowledge my transgressions: and my sin is ever before me" (Ps. 51:1–3).

No person could question David's sincerity, but unfortunately he pleased himself, and this was evident throughout his entire life. He always repented, but his remorse came too late to undo the damage done. His love for the Lord, the service rendered to

God's cause, and the serenity of his immortal sonnets fell through holes in the pocket of his soul. He was very wealthy and yet was too poor to purchase a moment of happiness.

It is never wise to be enamored with impurities. A desire for illegitimate pleasures of Egypt usually produces a longing to dwell there! Demas, the companion of Paul, lusted after the things of the world, and his craving became so intense, it ruined his service for Christ. Paul wrote: "Whatsoever things are true, whatsoever things are honest, whatsoever things are just, whatsoever things are pure, whatsoever things are lovely, whatsoever things are of good report; if there be any virtue, and if there be any praise, *think on these things*" (Phil. 4:8). Solomon said: "For as he thinketh in his heart, *so is he*" (Prov. 23:7). David's son was given great wisdom by God, but unfortunately he forgot to mend the hole in his pocket and became extremely foolish (see 1 Kings 11:1–4).

The Pocket of Appreciation

And not many days after the younger son gathered all together, and took his journey into a far country, and there wasted his substance with riotous living (Luke 15:13).

What a happy home is to a family, the church should be to the Christian. It has often been claimed that one never misses the water until the well runs dry, and that fact can be seen everywhere. It took a long time before the pigs became deplorable substitutes for the love of the prodigal's father. Sometimes it takes years before backsliding Christians recognize the privilege of belonging to the family of God. The best the world offers cannot satisfy the hungry souls of people who for a variety of reasons abandon the church. Occasionally, the church leaves much to be desired, but in spite of its problems, there is no place like home.

It was never revealed why the prodigal son desired to leave his family. Was he rebellious against his older brother? Did he dislike his father's attitude? Did he believe he could do better controlling his own destiny? The more he thought of his grievances, the larger became the hole in his pocket. Ultimately, he became so hungry and poor he began to steal the pigs' food. Only when he was impoverished, did the despised home appear to be the best place on earth. Someone said, "Sense bought is better than sense taught!" but that is a lesson hard to learn. If the prodigal son had known its truth, he might have repaired the hole in the pocket of his soul!

The Pocket of Attention

Behold, I come quickly; hold that fast which thou hast, *that no man take thy crown* (Rev. 3:11).

A stillborn child is one of the greatest tragedies in life. Similarly, a person who professes to be a Christian but never becomes active can only be a disappointment to God. Unfortunately, after spectacular evangelistic crusades many of the converts disappear. After widely publicized meetings in Los Angeles, workers who visited homes reported to the organizing committee. One said he had visited a certain family to encourage the converts to associate with a local church. He was disappointed when the man said, "Oh, no, we have done it, but that is enough. We do not wish to join a church, or have anything to do with the movement." According to the statistics compiled, many of the people who responded had holes in their pockets! Something of eternal value had fallen into oblivion.

Any soldier who enlists in the armed services and then disappears is accountable to the government. A person who professes to be a Christian and then ignores his responsibility leaves much to be desired. Conversion means commitment, and both the soldier and the Christian convert should know this fact. Jesus said, "If any man will come after me, let him deny himself, and take up his cross, and follow me" (Matt. 16:24).

No athlete ever won a crown when he quit the race before reaching the finishing post. I first learned that lesson when as a schoolboy I raced against another lad. I had the race won, but, believing I had a commanding lead, slowed down a few feet from the end of the race. My opponent overtook me and won by inches. "He that endureth to *the end*" is the man who obtains his crown. The Christians of Galatia made a similar mistake, for Paul said, "Ye did run well; who did hinder you that ye should not obey the truth?" (Gal. 5:7).

The Gospel of Christ not only offers pardon for the guilty; it promises crowns for the victors. When the Savior sent His message to the Christians in Philadelphia, He emphasized three vital issues.

1. A thought-provoking promise . . . *"Behold I come quickly"*
2. A tremendous plea . . . *"Hold fast that which thou hast"*
3. A terrible possibility . . . *"That no man take thy crown"*

The Lord could not have been promising an early return to earth. He was urging His followers to be faithful because their opportunity would soon end. Christ was reminding them of approaching death when service upon earth would cease. The time was short!

The Christians in Philadelphia had already earned a great reputation. Their work for the Lord had been wonderful. The Savior seemed to be warning them against "holes in their pockets." Neglect can be dangerous. The Lord was not suggesting they might lose their salvation. He had already said, "My sheep hear my voice, and I know them, and they follow me. And I give unto them eternal life; *and they shall never perish, neither shall any man pluck them out of my hand*" (John 10:27–28). It would be tragic to stand in the presence of Christ and be reminded of holes in the pockets! That should be something demanding immediate attention. Procrastination has always been the thief of time!

1. Ivor Powell, "Haggai and His Revival Crusade," *Bible Gems* (Grand Rapids: Kregel Publications, 1987), 87–88.

SECTION TWO
The New Testament

And going on from thence, he saw other two bretheren, James the son of Zebedee, and John his brother, in a ship with Zebedee their father, mending their nets; and he called them (Matt. 4:21).

And when his disciples James and John saw this, they said, Lord, wilt thou that we command fire to come down from heaven, and consume them, even as Elias did? (Luke 9:54).

And he killed James the brother of John with the sword (Acts 12:2).

It is interesting that three prominent members of the early church were known by the same name—James. (1) James, the brother of the Lord who later became the minister of the church in Jerusalem, and wrote the epistle bearing his name; (2) James the Less, or Younger (he was the son of one of the women called Mary, who was present when Christ was crucified, and (3) James, the son of Zebedee and brother of John (he is mentioned in the synoptic Gospels but not in the fourth Gospel). Perhaps John was reluctant to mention the exploits of his brother lest his motives be questioned. Yet it seems strange that additional information was not forthcoming, for James was one of the three faithful men who accompanied Jesus during the most intimate experiences of His life. All Christians know about Peter and John, but few seem to be aware of their companion. This study is an attempt to supply glimpses of James, the strong reliable man who never faltered during his association with the Savior.

A Sacred Duty . . . *Demanding*

He was the son of a very prosperous fisherman who lived near the Sea of Galilee. He and his brother John were probably junior partners in the family business, and it seems reasonable to believe they were associated with two other fishermen, Andrew and Simon. The fact that Zebedee employed "hired servants" suggests the business was very lucrative and well-known throughout the area (Mark 1:20). Zebedee was probably a very shrewd man who understood the temperament of his sons. John was a dreamer, a mother's boy, affectionate, thoughtful, and kind. James, on the other hand, was quiet, businesslike, and a parent's perfect successor to a retiring father. He knew about fishing and in the event of his parent's death could be depended upon to continue the family's tradition. The aging father loved and appreciated John but was intensely proud of the elder son in whose hands the family's future rested. James was a methodical man who could handle customers, scrutinize and make decisions regarding equipment. While John talked, James planned how best to improve the family's affairs. He understood boats, fishing conditions, and people. Zebedee was probably retained as an advisor. This preserved his dignity, self-esteem, and made him feel needed in the entire enterprise.

When John went off to hear a preacher from the wilderness, the father was not too surprised. That was to be expected of John who was interested in other things apart from fishing. Yet Zebedee was not too disturbed, for James was still there in charge of everything. Even when John returned with exciting news concerning a possible Messiah, the father was not too worried. The younger son was emotional, easily impressed, and impetuous. James, on the other hand, was dependable and practical, as solid as a rock. When John and James both announced their intention to leave their occupation to become assistants of the Preacher from Nazareth, old Zebedee was surprised, dismayed, and angry. Jesus had ruined his business and destroyed his family.

Many years ago, the Rev. Charles E. Guice, the pastor of the White Memorial Presbyterian Church in McComb, Mississippi, wrote a book entitled *The First Friends of the Best Friend*, and in it referred to another book *The Glorious Company*, written by co-authors Mygatt and Weatherspoon. Admittedly, the book was imaginative and fictitious, yet it might have been close to reality. They wrote: "Zebedee is not too surprised when John goes away to become a disciple of John the Baptist. A dreamer would do such a thing. The old man is a bit alarmed when John comes back with a new light in his eyes to tell James about a Man, called Jesus. Will John be able to persuade James to go? But he dismisses the idea; James is too practical. But James does decide to go and see about Jesus, and when he returns he has decided, to his father's dismay, to become a disciple. Why? The boy is leaving his business, his home, his future, his all. The old man is broken hearted, and refuses from that time to have anything to do with James. No, it isn't too fanciful. It rings true to what we know."[1]

A Sincere Disciple . . . *Departing*

> Now as he walked by the sea of Galilee, he saw Simon and Andrew his brother casting a net into the sea: for they were fishers. And Jesus said unto them, Come ye after me, and I will make you to become fishers of men. And straightway they forsook their nets, and followed him. And when he had gone a little further thence, he saw James the son of Zebedee, and John his brother, who also were in the ship mending their nets. And straightway he called them: and they left their father Zebedee in the ship with the hired servants, and went after him (Mark 1:16–20).

If Zebedee were dismayed and angry, he could hardly be blamed. To lose two sons in one morning was crippling to the business, home, and future. It was to be expected that James, John, and Simon, who had been associated in the fishing business, would continue their friendship in the company of Jesus, but it is difficult to understand why Andrew was excluded from the continuing fellowship. He was a soul winner, he liked people, and possibly was looking for potential converts while the other men slept.

It is important to remember the Savior called people who apparently were not talented. He used "little people" who, although they were not able to preach sermons as did Peter on the day of Pentecost, they nevertheless "stood up with him" when he confronted an angry mob. When Peter preached to the crowds in Jerusalem, he had no idea what reactions would follow. The people who had crucified Christ were about to murder Stephen, and were capable of terminating Simon's life. Nevertheless, whatever the consequences might be, James and his brethren courageously supported Peter and were ready to die with him or lead converts to Christ. They were the "small people," the insignificant Davids who were not afraid of Goliath.

A Strange Denial . . . *Disturbing*

> And it came to pass, when the time was come that he should be received up, he stedfastly set his face to go to Jerusalem,

116

And sent messengers before his face: and they went, and entered into a village of the Samaritans, to make ready for him. And they did not receive him, because his face was as though he would go to Jerusalem. And when his disciples James and John saw this, they said, Lord, wilt thou that we command fire to come down from heaven, and consume them, even as Elias did? But he turned, and rebuked them, and said, Ye know not what manner of spirit ye are of. For the Son of man is not come to destroy men's lives, but to save them. And they went to another village (Luke 9:51–56).

It might be easy to condemn James and John for their tempestuous outburst when the Samaritans refused to welcome Jesus into their village. Yet it is wise first to consider preceding events. They had just come from the Mount of Transfiguration where they had seen Moses and Elijah conversing with their master. Even the Lord's clothing had reflected the glory of God. Furthermore, a little earlier they had witnessed the overwhelming enthusiasm and gratitude of many Samaritans who declared to a woman of ill repute, "Now we believe, not because of thy saying: for we have heard him ourselves, and know that this is indeed the Christ, the Savior of the world" (John 4:42). Evidently James was deeply disturbed, but believed that if he were given permission, he could emulate the action of the famous prophet and call down fire from heaven. The unfriendly attitude of the despised Samaritans was a terrible contrast to the enthusiasm of their kinsfolk in Sychar. On the spur of the moment, James decided it would be wonderful if they paid for their unfriendliness. Yet, when Jesus restrained the false enthusiasm, James did not argue. He accepted the authority of his Master, and accompanied Him to another village. The fact that Jesus called them "The Sons of Thunder" seems to indicate, "they were men of like passions as we are."

James was a loyal man; he never backed down from any challenges. He never ran. If it were necessary, he would confront not only men from a Samaritan village. He would also defy the hosts of hell. Other disciples denied, one betrayed his leader, and at times all wavered a little, but James was the man who stood firm, atoned for failure, and then resumed his service for Christ.

117

A Special Desire . . . *Disgusting*

Then came to him the mother of Zebedee's children with her
sons, worshiping him, and desiring a certain thing of him. And
he said unto her, What wilt thou? She saith unto him, Grant that
these my two sons, may sit, the one on thy right hand, and the
other on the left, in thy kingdom (Matt. 20:20–21).

Peter, James, and John! We know a great deal about two of
them. Peter was always prominent among the disciples and was
greatly used by the Holy Spirit on the day of Pentecost. He also
wrote two letters that are included in the Scriptures. John was
famous in his own right, and he also wrote five books which are
in the Bible. But what is known of James? There is very little
except that he was involved in a scheme to secure seats of honor
within the kingdom of Christ. There is not any evidence that
James was responsible for the request made to Jesus. Probably it
was the result of a devoted mother desiring the best for her
children. Perhaps James and John agreed to her suggestion because of their profound respect for their parent. What little is
known of James does not support the idea that he would seek
notoriety at the expense of his brethren. He was the faithful,
untiring man who became one of the leaders of the church. Unfortunately, the assemblies were soon deprived of his guidance—
for Herod the king, in an attempt to destroy the new movement,
decided to murder the fearless Christian. All people are susceptible to praise, but there are still those within the church who
continue to serve Christ even though they are never mentioned
in any pulpit. They are the strong, reliable souls upon whom the
Lord depends and without whom the church would never grow.

A Saddening Death . . . *Dismaying*

Now about that time Herod the king stretched forth his hand
to vex certain of the church. And he killed James the brother
of John with the sword (Acts 12:1–2).

It is significant that Herod attacked James and Peter, but for
reasons unknown, John was never apprehended. Luke recorded
the deliverance of Simon Peter (Acts 12), but the other son of
Zebedee laid down his life for the Savior. Evidently the authorities of those days recognized James to be a leader of the new

118

movement and hoped his demise would cause irreparable harm. Eusebius, an early historian of Christianity, tells a remarkable story which he claimed had been handed down from a lost work of Clement of Alexandria. It tells how the informer against James was so impressed by the testimony of the apostle before his judge, that he also became a Christian and they died together. On the way to their execution, the accuser asked for forgiveness, and after a moment's hesitation, James said: "Peace be with thee," and then kissed him.[2]

James is the apostle of insignificant men and women. The Irish folk revere St. Patrick and the Welsh, St. David, but the citizens of all countries who feel forgotten and neglected can look with pride to the apostle James, who sealed his testimony with his blood. He surely had a great welcome when he rejoined his Lord in the land of endless day.

1. Charles, E. Guick, *The First Friends of the Best Friend* (Morrilton, Mississippi: Morrilton Democrat, 1932), 74.

2. *The Pulpit Commentary,* vol. 18 (Grand Rapids: Eerdmans, 1950), 369.

MATTHEW-LEVI—WHO DID
NOT WISH TO FORGET HIS PAST

*And as Jesus passed forth from thence, he saw a man, named
Matthew, sitting at the receipt of custom: and he saith unto
him, Follow me. And he arose, and followed him. And it came
to pass as Jesus sat at meat in the house, behold, many
publicans and sinners came and sat down with him
and his disciples (Matt. 9:9–10).*

*And after these things he [Jesus] went forth, and saw a
publican, named Levi, sitting at the receipt of custom: and he
said unto him, Follow me. . . . And Levi made him a great feast
in his own house: and there was a great company of publicans and of others that sat down with them (Luke 5:27, 29).*

The first three Gospels are known as "The Synoptic Gospels"
because for the most part they describe the same events. The
word *synoptic* is derived from two Greek words and means "giving or constituting a general view" or "presenting the same or
similar point of view." It is the name given to the first three
Gospels. All students know that the gospels of Matthew, Mark,
and Luke basically describe identical events, and often the expressions of the three authors have a remarkable resemblance. It
is true that each writer had a point to prove and an individualis-
tic way of achieving his purpose. Matthew-Levi, a Jew, firmly
believed Jesus to be the Messiah, and endeavored to prove this
to his Hebrew readers. Mark set out to portray the Savior of
Simon Peter, and consequently his gospel is one of continuing
action. Luke, who obtained much of his material from Paul and
other early Christians, set out to prove that Jesus was indeed the
God-Man, perfect in every detail of His humanity. To repeat,
each author had his own method of reaching his literary goal.
Nevertheless, it must be remembered that only Matthew had
been a traveling companion of the Lord. He alone of the three
writers could claim to have been an eyewitness of the things
described in his book.[1]

It is interesting to note that the call of Matthew and the feast
arranged for the Savior are mentioned in all the synoptic Gospels.
Yet there is a subtle difference in the records, which may or may

not be significant. Matthew is believed to have possessed two names. Matthew might have been the name given at his birth; Levi could have been given by the Savior. The Lord gave a second name to Simon, and it is possible He did the same for Matthew. It is fascinating that Mark and Luke never referred to their colleague as Matthew—*the publican.* When they spoke of their fellow worker, they used the name Levi (see Luke 5:27). When Matthew referred to himself, he was careful to emphasize that he collected taxes for the detestable Romans. That fact elicits questions.

To Produce Humility

Did Matthew persist in the use of this title so that he would be reminded constantly of his indebtedness to the Savior? Unfortunately some people advertise their misdeeds of former years. They magnify their sins to produce a sensational testimony, and draw attention to themselves! Matthew had no personal claim to fame. He was not an eloquent speaker such as Peter or John. He was a man of books, a collector of facts, a person accustomed to keeping records. There was nothing particularly glamorous about his work, but it needed patience and accuracy. While his brethren were busy working with people, Matthew wrote his manuscript. Had he been less faithful, the world would not now possess Matthew's gospel. Did he ever become weary, feeling his work was unimportant? When he saw his writings increase, was he tempted to believe his efforts would be of more value than the preaching of his colleagues? The answers to these questions cannot be known, but Matthew was determined to be remembered as *the publican.* He who had been detestable had been brought into a glorious fellowship. Old things had passed away and everything had become new. He owed everything to Christ and wished his readers to be aware of that fact.

Mark and Luke referred to him as Levi. Is it possible that they were a little ashamed of Matthew's past? Many Jews remembered that he had collected taxes and, as it has often been said, "Give someone a bad name, and he has it forever." Were they afraid his former employment would prevent his success as a disciple of Christ, and for that reason, used his less provocative name? A comparison of the biblical records is interesting.

To Prevent Haughtiness

It has been claimed there are two sides to every picture, and that applies to the present problem. Humility and pride do not belong in the same family. Matthew possessed a rare gift—he was a man of books.

Apart from John there was not another man capable of doing Matthew's work. John basically was a fisherman. He eventually wrote his gospel because he realized other writers had omitted facts essential in the story of Jesus. John *became* a book man. Matthew had always been one. The other disciples were interested in miracles, and it is doubtful whether they had sufficient patience to collect and tabulate the facts necessary to complete a book.

Perhaps as his fame increased, and his writings circulated among the churches, Matthew gained for himself a place of eminence in the esteem of his readers. This might have become a source of pride. Paul wrote: "For I say, through the grace given unto me, to every man that is among you, not to think of himself more highly than he ought to think; but to think soberly, according as God hath dealt to every man the measure of faith" (Rom. 12:3). Was Matthew aware of this danger and, to prevent its becoming a menace, reminding himself of what he was before he met the Savior?

Success is sometimes a temptation hard to overcome. Every man is susceptible to flattery, and unfortunately many people have failed to achieve their goals because they became self-made deities who worshiped at their own shrine. Some churches lost their effectiveness because they believed themselves to be the only authentic interpreters of theology. It is generally a safe rule that if a man claims to be God's only spokesman, avoid him. Arguments provide strife in which fellowship with other Christians becomes impossible. Paul said: "Let nothing be done through strife or vainglory; but in lowliness of mind let each esteem others better than themselves" (Phil. 2:3). The same idea was expressed by the Savior when He said:

> When thou art bidden of any man to a wedding, sit not down in the highest room; lest a more honourable man than thou be bidden of him; And he that bade thee and him come and say to thee, Give this man place; and thou begin with shame to

122

take the lowest room. But when thou art bidden, go and sit down in the lowest room; that when he that bade thee cometh, he may say unto thee, Friend, go up higher: then shalt thou have worship in the presence of them that sit at meat with thee. For whosoever exalted himself shall be abased; and he that humbleth himself shall be exalted (Luke 14:8–11).

Matthew did what had been recommended by the Savior and demonstrated he was not only a talented writer, he was also an excellent listener.

To Provide Help

When Matthew insisted he had been a publican, was he thinking of others of his type? It was significant that his first act as a disciple was to arrange a feast to which he invited many publicans and sinners. Evidently he believed that what Christ had done for him could be done for others. He desired to introduce his associates to his new Friend. When the delivered demoniac of Gadara was refused permission to accompany Jesus on His journey, he was commissioned to go home and tell everybody what had happened to him (Luke 8:38–39). Matthew did not need to be told; he made arrangements that Jesus would have the opportunity to speak for Himself.

It has often been claimed that news travels fast, but its speed was never greater than on that memorable day when Matthew became host for folk considered to be untouchables! As was to be expected, the religious leaders criticized the Lord for associating with such people. A large party would not terminate within minutes; the meal was the best money could provide. When the guests had eaten, Matthew, the Master of Ceremonies, introduced his Guest, and responding, the Lord addressed the audience. It would be interesting to know what He said. If only someone had possessed a tape recorder! That gathering was a forerunner of all the evangelistic meetings for which the early church became famous. The host, whose eyes shone with delight, agreed with everything spoken and, when the opportunity presented itself, would exclaim to the listeners, "I told you. I knew that if the Lord could do this for me, He would do it for you."

There is no evidence that Matthew ever became a great preacher. It is said that on the Day of Pentecost the other disciples

123

stood up with Simon Peter. At that time no one knew what the final result would be. The angry crowds had just crucified the Lord and would soon murder Stephen, but no one could have known that between those events thousands of people would enter the kingdom of God. Matthew and his brethren risked their lives when they stood with their colleague. Peter preached; they prayed! Matthew loved to help in any way possible and to that end dedicated his talents and money. He began placing his notes in order, and eventually his gospel made its appearance. Scribes made copies of the manuscript, and as the book began to circulate among the churches, people increasingly appreciated its author.

Did he ever imagine what his work would accomplish? Did he know that kings and queens, educated and illiterate, millionaires and paupers, and people from every level of society would admire Matthew the publican? If saints in heaven know what happens on earth, he must be proud that he was the man with a pen! He who supplied a meal for his publican friends has satisfied the spiritual hunger and thirst of all Christians. It would not be surprising if, when Matthew is introduced in heaven, he interrupts the proceedings to say, "Brother, don't forget to tell them I am Matthew, *the publican*."

---

1.   Ivor Powell, *Matthew's Majestic Gospel* (Grand Rapids: Kregel Publications, 1986), 13.

It has often been said that good things come in small packages. It may also be claimed that sublime truth is often expressed in simple words. I once heard a theological student say his greatest ambition as a preacher would be to shower his congregation with the spray from an oceanic vocabulary! That young man devoted time each day to the learning and use of new words. Most ministers would prefer to utter one meaningful sentence than to speak for an hour and say nothing. Christians believe that Jesus was the Master of everything—including speech. Had He desired, He could have delivered orations that would have dumbfounded the most educated Pharisees. When the Lord spoke, "they were astonished and said, Whence hath this man this wisdom, and these mighty works? Is not this the carpenter's son? Is not his mother called Mary? and his brethren, James and Joseph, and Simon, and Judas? And his sisters, are they not all with us? Whence then hath this man all these things?" (Matt. 13:54–56).

It seems strange that one of the longest words Jesus used was "whosoever," and the one He liked best was "Come." He invited His disciples to "come and see" (John 1:39), "come and drink" (John 7:37), "come and dine" (John 21:12).[1] The Lord asked all kinds of people to come, and some of the Bible's most delightful stories describe folk who gladly accepted His invitation. Even before babies understand words, they recognize the meaning conveyed by the outstretched arms of a mother. Constantly Jesus had pleasure in asking people to come to Him, and He has never changed. A simple acrostic is self-explanatory—Christ Offers Me Everything.

Come and Rest

Come unto me, all ye that labour and are heavy laden, and I will give you rest (Matt. 11:28).

This challenging promise was one of the Lord's greatest statements. If there were nothing more to support His claim to deity, this brief utterance would be enough.

Consider Its Simplicity . . . "Come"

I have seen people in India and other parts of the world attempting to perform the impossible, and when I asked why they did such things, I was told, "I hope to please God and be forgiven." Pilgrims travel to distant shrines, desperate men flog themselves in their search for peace, and every Easter men in the Philippines are crucified in the hope of obtaining forgiveness. The Savior said, "Come unto me," and this is possible at any time, in any part of the world. There is no charge to pay, no promise to make, and nothing to do except *come*.

Consider Its Scope . . . "All"

"All ye that labour and are heavy laden." Oppression, misery, and despondency afflict all people. Money cannot buy everything and sorrow invades the life of everybody. The doors of a palace cannot exclude it; great wealth cannot prevent it. Education may influence a man's mind but cannot guarantee immunity from grief. Unrest is universal, therefore the promise of Christ was meant for all people irrespective of creed, color, or nationality.

Consider Its Sufficiency . . . "Rest"

Jesus said, "I will give you rest." Wise men offer advice and wealthy people financial assistance, but only Jesus can give rest. The Savior is able to relieve a tortured conscience and calm a troubled soul. Jesus of Nazareth has been approached by millions of distressed souls, and not one came to Him in vain. The same love that welcomed children cares for the sick, the aged, and the dying.

Come and Renew

And the apostles gathered themselves together unto Jesus, and told him all things, both what they had done, and what they had taught. And he said unto them, Come ye yourselves apart into a desert place, and rest awhile: for there were many coming and going, and they had no leisure so much as to eat (Mark 6:30–32).

The disciples were enthusiastic. They had completed their missionary itinerary but could hardly believe what had been accomplished. Sick people had been healed, the blind given sight, and the response to their teaching had been phenomenal. Large crowds had attended their meetings, but now they were in danger of overestimating their own importance. Satan had been given the greatest shock of his life! "Lord," they exclaimed, "even the devils were subject unto us!"

Jesus smiled. He knew them better than they knew themselves. To use modern terms, their lights were shining brightly, but they were in danger of draining their batteries! Crowds of people were waiting expectantly, questions were being asked, and sick folk were clamoring for attention. There was no time for a meal! The Lord said, "Follow me," and led them to a secluded place in the wilderness. His followers were shocked. "Master, the devil is almost vanquished. Let's finish him off before he recovers. If God be for us, who can be against us? A couple more days and our followers will exceed the Romans. The kingdom can be established, and you will be the King of Kings." The Savior probably answered, "Sit down and enjoy your food." He was calm and peaceful; it appeared He had all the time in the world. "Master, what about the lame and the blind and the others?" He replied, "What about them? They will be here tomorrow. Just lie down, take a deep breath and dream about the future." Then as darkness began to cover the area, he fell asleep, and with nothing left to do, they emulated His example. Jesus was trying to impart wisdom to men whose enthusiasm could be dangerous. It is unwise to burn a candle at both ends! The disciples needed to learn that lesson. When Christ commands people to work, it is sinful to disobey. When He says, "Stop and rest," it is foolish to work harder. Satan does not resent people working for the Lord—as long as their labor is ineffective. He prefers to attend their funeral than to listen to their testimony. Unfortunately, many of God's children work until they drop. They forget the command: "Be still and know that I am God." Excessive work leads to stress, tension, irritability, and anger. People become upset. It is difficult to live with them and remain undisturbed. They hurt other people, and their happiness is ruined. The only cure for that kind of sickness is to go out into the country with God—and stay there until the fever subsides. Some young preachers cannot understand how the church existed for almost two thousand years without their aid! Every Christian worker needs to recharge his batteries by being connected continually to the Source of all power. The poet said: "Oh, to be nothing, nothing, simply to lie at His feet. A broken and emptied vessel for the Master's use made meet."

Come and Reason

Come now, and let us reason together, saith the LORD: though your sins be as scarlet, they shall be as white as snow; though they be red like crimson, they shall be as wool (Isa. 1:18).

Isaiah preached during the reign of four kings, but his counsel had a mixed reception. Uzziah, Jothan, and Hezekiah did that which was right in the sight of the Lord, but Ahaz pleased himself. Unfortunately, the nation tried to walk in two directions at the same time and succeeded in getting nowhere! They professed to love God but worshiped idols and offered incense in the shrines of the nation.

I have nourished and brought up children, and they have rebelled against me. The ox knoweth his owner, and the ass his master's crib: but Israel doth not know, my people doth not consider (Isa. 1:2–3).

How Fair

Had Israel been rejected, they could not have complained; they were unfaithful. God had treated them as His children, but they had been rebellious. The animals were more intelligent than their owners. They knew how to return to their stalls, but the Jews forgot their Benefactor. Nevertheless, the Lord was willing to consider their complaints and pardon their behavior. He invited them to consider what they had done. He was the giver of every good and perfect gift, but Israel remained ungrateful.

How Fortunate

"I have nourished and brought up *children*." Israel had not been strangers to the Almighty; they belonged to His family. Throughout their history they had been protected from enemies; there were no reasons to justify their conduct; God would listen and do what He could to correct their grievances. It was extremely fortunate for the tribes that it could be said: "Like as a father pitieth his children, so the LORD pitieth them that fear him" (Ps. 103:13). If God had not sustained His people, they would have perished. God's love was indestructible, and that is true today. To those who have lost their fellowship, He continues to say, "Return, ye backsliding children, and I will heal your backslidings" (Jer. 3:22).

". . . though your sins be as scarlet, they shall be as white as snow; though they be red like crimson, they shall be as wool."

It is difficult to understand the greatness of God's mercy. Our tolerance of sinners would not equal His. Jehovah was considered to be a harsh and frightening God. To believe Him to be a Father welcoming sinners was something new. God was not an austere deity waiting to pounce upon transgressors. He was, as Jesus described, the Father of prodigals.

Come and Rejoice

Then shall the king say unto them on his right hand, Come, ye blessed of my Father, inherit the kingdom prepared for you from the foundation of the world (Matt. 25:34).

At the end of his career Paul wrote: "Henceforth there is laid up for me a crown of righteousness, which the Lord, the righteous judge shall give me at that day: and not to me only, but unto all them also that love his appearing" (2 Tim. 4:8). Among the nations of the world it is customary after any great victory for the participating soldiers to parade before their commander-in-chief. Some men who distinguished themselves on the field of battle are given the highest honors offered by their country. Paul believed the greatest of all parades will take place "when the saints go marching in."

Unfortunately not all Christians will be rewarded for gallantry. The apostle expected to be given a crown of righteousness, and John, writing to the churches of Asia, mentioned other crowns available to those who earn them. The Savior was definitive when He spoke about a kingdom prepared and planned from before the beginning of time. It was surprising that he spoke of feeding the hungry, giving water to thirsty people, clothing the naked, visiting the sick, and helping people in prison. He said these were the deeds meriting rewards. He never mentioned dynamic preaching, great fame within the church, convincing oratory, or generous gifts to worthy organizations.

Then shall the righteous answer him saying, Lord, when saw we thee an hungred, and fed thee? or thirsty, and gave thee drink? When saw we thee a stranger, and took thee in? or

129

naked, and clothed thee? Or when saw we thee sick, or in prison, and came unto thee? And the King shall answer and say unto them, Verily I say unto you, Inasmuch as ye have done it unto one of the least of these my brethren, ye have done it unto me (Matt. 25:37–40).

Many people will be surprised when they stand before the throne of God. Some who expect great recognition may be disappointed. Others anticipating nothing, may receive crowns. When Christ spoke about that glittering occasion, He introduced his message by saying, "*Come*, ye blessed of my Father, inherit the kingdom prepared for you from the foundation of the world." Blessed are they who can confidently say:

> Oh that will be glory for me, glory for me, glory for me;
> When by His grace I shall look on His face,
> That will be glory, be glory for me.

1. Ivor Powell, *John's Wonderful Gospel* (Grand Rapids: Kregel Publications, 1986), 44–46.

WHEN YOUR WORLD IS
FALLING APART—TELL JESUS

*And [John's] disciples came, and took up the body, and
buried it, and went and told Jesus (Matt. 14:12).*

The Problem of Doubt . . . *How Disturbing* (Luke 7:19)

The disciples of John the Baptist had just made a terrible
discovery. They had come to Herod's prison to converse with
their leader, but had been horrified to see a bloodstained body
which indicated the cell had become an execution chamber.
The head of the evangelist had been given to a dancing girl,
while the decapitated body lay on the dusty floor. As the men
unashamedly wept, their world of expectation and hope
collapsed, and they probably wished they had died with their
master. Eighteen months earlier, they had been impressed by
the wilderness preacher. His clarion call for repentance had
stirred the conscience of the nation, and believing him to be the
anointed of God, they left all to become his disciples. John did
not perform any physical miracles, but his message brought
spiritual health to the multitudes who attended the meetings in
the Jordan valley. It had seemed then that the Kingdom of God
was near. Every day those men assisted at baptisms and
counseled converts. The normal routine of daily living seemed
to be far away when they attended to the needs of their new
friend. They were stirred when they heard his fearless
denunciation of hypocrisy, then charmed when his eyes became
pools of compassion. He seldom, if ever, visited the temple, for
he appeared to enjoy perpetual access to the Almighty. The
prophet was amazing, sincere, fearless—he was marvelous.

Their earlier occupations were forgotten. Perhaps they were
fishermen or farmers, married or single, young or old, but they
were attracted to a man whose vision encompassed eternity. They
became known as the disciples of John. Their numbers were
never revealed. Perhaps there were others who would have shared
the privilege, but business or family responsibilities prevented
their doing so. When John addressed the daily audiences, his
friends were spellbound. They had never heard such a convincing
preacher. When many people responded to the teaching of their
leader, the disciples were proud they had a part in the ministry.

131

A smile from John was sunrise to their souls. To sit at his feet and share a frugal meal seemed to be fellowship with God.

And then one day came the strange Man from Galilee. He was courteous, reverent, and sincere, yet he was unlike their own master. He seemed like a royal prince, but his hands were rough from hard labor. John was strangely moved when the Visitor requested baptism, and the congregation was fascinated when a dove flew down to sit on the Candidate's shoulder. It was a sign from heaven that God was pleased with the proceedings. But soon unforeseen events brought frowns to the faces of those disciples. John and Andrew had been charmed by the Carpenter from Nazareth and had forsaken the fellowship. They betrayed a trust and gave their support to another leader. That was unpardonable. As time passed, it became evident that John's popularity was subsiding. He never performed miracles, but Jesus was healing the sick, giving sight to the blind, and cleansing lepers. People were unreliable and disappointing. How could they support another preacher when their own master needed help? He who had stirred the conscience of Israel was now fading into obscurity. They were shocked to hear that Jesus dined with publicans and sinners. Their master had urged people to flee from the wrath to come. Something was wrong! To fraternize with self-righteous hypocrites could not be pleasing to the Almighty. Yet John never complained. One day he tried to explain that Jesus would increase while he would decrease, but they could not understand why this should be so. Their dislike of the situation was hard to hide.

Then things took a turn for the worse. The excitement disappeared. The people attending John's services were few. It was disappointing to see the crowds attending the services of the Preacher from Galilee. Suddenly John appeared to be sidetracked. Instead of concentrating on his meetings, he began denouncing King Herod. When he was arrested and imprisoned, the disciples shook their heads and murmured, "We are not surprised. Now we have no services at all." Yet unlike John and Andrew who had left the fellowship, the other disciples remained true to their imprisoned leader and were determined to stay with him whatever happened. It was difficult to understand why Jesus was prospering when their beloved leader was facing death. Had God ceased to care about righteousness? The question demanded an answer, for doubt was spreading as a cancer through their souls.

During one of the visits to the prison John recognized they had a problem, and ultimately the men explained what was troubling them. "Master, do you remember that Carpenter from Nazareth whom you baptized? You told us that He was the Messiah who would take away the sins of the world. Were you mistaken? A more unlikely Messiah would be hard to find. He is certainly not following in your footsteps. You told sinners to flee from the wrath to come, but he is dining with them and having a great time. We expected Him to expel our oppressors, but Jesus is telling everybody to love their enemies. Master, is it possible that you were mistaken, and should we begin looking for another leader?"

John was very still. His thoughts had returned to the meetings when God did such amazing things, when crowds watched as the Stranger from Galilee was immersed. It is not known how long he deliberated, but suddenly he sighed and said, "Go to Jesus and tell Him that I sent you. Ask Him, 'Art thou he that should come? or look we for another?'" (Luke 7:19). He knew the disciples' problem could not be solved by any answer he could supply. Jesus would know how to handle the situation. "Yes, my brothers, go and tell Jesus about your difficulties." When they arrived, the Lord listened to their question and delayed His answer until He had finished healing the sick. "Then Jesus answering said unto them, Go your way, and tell John what things ye have seen and heard; how that the blind see, the lame walk, the lepers are cleansed, the deaf hear, the dead are raised, to the poor the gospel is preached. And blessed is he, whosoever shall not be offended in me" (Luke 7:22–23).

As the messengers returned to John's prison, they reflected upon what they had seen and heard. Who was He? No man could do the things He did unless God were with Him. After their departure the Lord paid John his greatest compliment. "What went ye out into the wilderness for to see? A reed shaken with the wind? . . . I say unto you, Among those that are born of women there is not a greater prophet than John the Baptist" (Luke 7:24–28). The prophet was not a victim of unbelief. He was not confident one day and doubtful the next. He was completely reliable. When he received their report, he smiled and knew the Lord had met the need of his friends.

Then came the moment when those disciples looked at the

headless body of their leader. Gently they carried his body to its last resting place and buried their friend. Perhaps they made a simple marker to place on the grave. Someone said, "What can we do now?" and a disciple answered, "Let's go and tell Jesus. There is nothing else we can do." Any grievance against John and Andrew was forgotten. They had ceased looking at men and thought only of Jesus. They looked at the grave of John and then began their journey to meet Christ. They were welcomed, and their night ended when the Sun of Righteousness arose "with healing in His wings" (Mal. 4:2).

The best thing to do when one's world is falling apart, when hopes and plans are ruined and no one understands our problems, is to go and tell Jesus. The gospel singers say it best: "Steal away, steal away; steal away to Jesus." If the events recorded by Luke are chronologically correct, two of his references are most illuminating. He tells us in the seventh chapter of his gospel that after the burial of their master the disciples went and told Jesus everything. Later in chapter 10 he describes how the Savior's original twelve disciples had increased to seventy. Were the disciples of John included in that number? It seems to be a safe conclusion that those weary men found a new meaning to life when they shared their sorrow with the Lord.

The Problem of Delight . . . *How Dangerous* (Luke 10:17)

Other New Testament characters shared their experience. The seventy preachers were ecstatic with joy when they returned from the missionary journey. They said, "Lord, even the devils are subject unto us through thy name" (Luke 10:17). A trail of blessedness had been left behind. Miracles had been performed by the touch of their hands. Without any special training those untutored men accomplished the impossible. Their fame would spread throughout the land; they would be welcomed in every community; their future was assured. Were they surprised when the Lord said, "Rejoice not, that the spirits are subject unto you; but rather rejoice, because your names are written in heaven" (Luke 10:20). The popular chorus seems to express what He was trying to say. "To know your sins are all forgiven is something more than gold."

The Problem of Disappointment . . . *How Deluding* (John 11:6)

Mary and Martha were devastated by the serious illness of

Lazarus. It was evident the local physicians were incapable of curing his sickness. As they sat beside the bed of their brother, they remembered the amazing ability of their friend Jesus. "Therefore his sisters sent unto him, saying, Lord, behold, he whom thou lovest is sick" (John 11:3). They sought the assistance of a friend or neighbor but became confused and disappointed when Jesus failed to respond immediately. Eventually they discovered there was wisdom in all the Lord's actions. When Jesus came to their home He not only restored Lazarus to life, He taught the women to know the value of complete trust in God.

The Problem of Disgrace . . . *How Depressing* (Luke 24:34)

Simon Peter hated himself, for he had disgraced his calling and disowned his Master. His conscience troubled him. He could not explain the madness which had brought condemnation to his soul. Somewhere in the darkness he wept bitterly. Life had ended. He could never again face his brethren. Perhaps he was unaware that the Lord had sent a special message to him. The angel at the tomb said: "Be not afraid: Ye seek Jesus of Nazareth, which was crucified; he is risen; he is not here: behold the place where they laid him. But go your way, tell his disciples *and Peter* that he goeth before you into Galilee: there shall ye see him, as he said unto you" (Mark 16:6–7). Poor Simon! He was ashamed of his behavior and was too embarrassed to meet the Lord. It seems evident that Jesus thought it necessary to go in search of the wayward disciple. When the travelers returned unexpectedly from Emmaus, they heard how the Lord had appeared to Simon (Luke 24:34).

Somewhere in the city the Lord came to Peter, and placing a hand upon his shoulder, asked: "Did you not receive my message?" Peter lowered his head, for he was too ashamed to look into the Savior's face. Perhaps they wept together when Peter confessed his shameful unworthiness. He told the Master everything. He did not know then that he was destined to become one of God's most successful servants.

Most of God's people considered themselves to be failures, but they knew the value of conversing with Christ. Wise people transform failures into stepping stones. When one's world is falling apart, it is wise to tell Jesus.

During the years when I was the evangelist of the Baptist

135

Church in Canada, my schedule of meetings was so exhausting that it became necessary to seek medical assistance. A wonderful doctor in the city of Lethbridge, Alberta, welcomed me to his office and for two days subjected me to many tests. He belonged to the church and attended meetings almost every night. Ultimately, he sat at his desk, smiled, and said, "I am happy to tell you that there is nothing organically wrong with you. You have been working too hard, and since you must preach every night, you must cancel some of the day meetings." He told me of certain foods that could be harmful to my health, and finally said, "Ivor Powell, you are a doctor of the soul. I am a doctor of the body. In the church I listen to you. Here, you must listen to me. Go out into the country and sit down under a tree with God. You will feel better, you will be better, and you'll preach better." His advice not only helped me physically—it led to some of the most wonderful experiences of my life. I did as he advised. That was forty years ago, and thank God, I am still preaching. It is wise to talk with the Lord.

Then Jesus went thence, and departed into the coasts of Tyre and Sidon. And, behold, a woman of Canaan came out of the same coasts, and cried unto him, saying, Have mercy on me, O Lord, thou Son of David; my daughter is grievously vexed with a devil (Matthew 15:21–22).

And it came to pass the day after, that he went into a city called Nain; and many of his disciples went with him, and much people. Now when he came nigh to the gate of the city, behold, there was a dead man carried out, the only son of his mother, and she was a widow: and much people of the city was with her (Luke 7:11–12).

He left Judea, and departed again into Galilee. And he must needs go through Samaria. Then cometh he to a city of Samaria, which is called Sychar, near to the parcel of ground that Jacob gave to his son Joseph. Now Jacob's well was there. Jesus therefore, being wearied with his journey, sat thus on the well: and it was about the sixth hour (John 4:3–6).

It is interesting to discover that although the Savior visited certain places many times, there were others to which He only went once. It may be difficult to explain His actions, but always the special journey led to an extraordinary event. The center of Christ's ministry was indisputably in Galilee, and probably in the city of Capernaum where He preached many of His sermons. Jesus was also a frequent visitor to Bethany, and, since that village was only six miles from Jerusalem, it may be assumed He often visited the city of David. Perhaps He made repeated visits to other places, but it may be significant that the Bible mentions only one visit to Tyre and Sidon, Sychar's Well, and the city of Nain. Apparently the Lord made special efforts to reach those areas, because in each place was a woman urgently needing assistance. The three occasions supply evidence of His concern for distressed people.

The Determined Woman ... *Acting*

Then Jesus went thence, and departed into the coasts of Tyre and Sidon. And behold a woman of Canaan came out of the same coasts, and cried unto him, saying, Have mercy on me, O Lord, thou Son of David; my daughter is grievously vexed with a devil (Matt. 15:21–22).

The Syrophenician woman was very apprehensive, for she was about to attempt the impossible! Jesus, the Healer from Nazareth, was approaching her city, and, in the presence of a great crowd of spectators, she planned to become an actress. Later when she reminisced, the folly of her attempt would become apparent, but she was desperate. Her daughter's life was in danger.

She had often watched the crowds going south to attend the great meetings in Capernaum and had heard many testimonies of Christ's ability to assist afflicted people. Her neighbors always emphasized the Preacher was a Jew, and their attitude reminded her she was a Gentile, an outsider, a dog! Nevertheless, the condition of her child—possibly recurring attacks of epilepsy—was deteriorating. It was said the sickness was related to demon possession and was incurable. Capernaum was about one hundred miles to the south of her home. She had no transportation, and it was unwise either to leave her girl or expect the afflicted daughter to travel that distance. Then one day she heard that Jesus was about to visit her city. Could it be possible that He would help her? The Jews would be indignant at the suggestion, but when she considered the possibility, she became excited. The Man from the south did not know her. If she dressed as did the Jewesses in her community it might be possible to deceive Him. She spoke Hebrew fluently. Her plans to deceive the Lord were pathetic, but sincere.

The crowds were jostling each other for better viewpoints and the Lord was smiling as His party approached the anxious mother. Suddenly, her electrifying cry echoed down the street. "Jesus, thou Son of David, have mercy on me." Her request was apparently unheard as the Lord continued speaking to His friends. The disciples were embarrassed as they whispered, "Master, if you do not intend to help her, send her away. People are watching and listening. This is not a good start to our visit." He replied, "I am not sent but unto the lost sheep of the house of Israel." She instantly replied, "If you are sent to the lost sheep of the house of Israel, *help me.*" Maybe the Lord sighed; she had continued her effort to deceive Him. She was a Gentile, and was not a

138

descendant of David. Her initial request "Thou son fo Daivd" was an affront to the Hebrew heritage. Her second request indicated she had passed the point of no return. "Woman, it is not meet to take the children's bread and to cast it to dogs."

The mother trembled, for she had failed in her task. No person could deceive Jesus. He understood her inmost thoughts. Her hair was probably touching the ground when that realization overwhelmed her soul. Then suddenly, she put back her head, looked into His face, and said, "Truth, Lord: yet the dogs eat of the crumbs which fall from their masters' table." Even the angels might have smiled when Christ replied, "O woman, great is thy faith: be it unto thee even as thou wilt." And her daughter was made whole from that very hour. "Of course, little lady. I shall be thrilled to grant your request, but that could not be done until you were honest both with yourself and with Me."

Then a strange thing happened. "Peter, John, all of you, let us return." There is no record that Jesus performed any other miracle nor addressed any audience in the area. Apparently His only reason for visiting Tyre and Sidon was to meet that devoted mother. The next verse in Matthew's gospel says: "And Jesus departed from thence, and came nigh unto the sea of Galilee; and went up into a mountain, and sat down there. And great multitudes came unto him" (Matt. 15:29). This was His only visit to Tyre and Sidon. Temporarily He had abandoned the crowded meetings in Capernaum to visit a helpless woman who lived one hundred miles away. How great were His perception, patience, and power.[1]

The Defiled Woman . . . *Asking*

Perhaps the disciples of Christ were disturbed as they trudged along behind their Master. The day was disgustingly hot, the atmosphere heavy and oppressive, and the dust disturbed by many feet clung as a thin layer of cement to their perspiring faces. Every sensible citizen was about to enjoy a siesta, and even the dogs were beginning to sleep. Why the Lord could not wait a few hours until traveling conditions improved was difficult to understand!

"And [Jesus] must needs go through Samaria. Then cometh he to a city of Samaria, which is called Sychar, near to the parcel of ground that Jacob gave to his son Joseph. Now Jacob's well was there. Jesus therefore, being wearied with his journey, sat thus on

139

the well: and it was about the sixth hour" (John 4:4–6). The disciples looked at the nearby city and made their excuses to leave. It was lunch time. They were hungry. The shops would soon be closing for several hours. Provisions were needed! It is not known how many disciples were with the Lord on this occasion, but in any case, one man could have purchased all that was needed. That they all went into the city indicated their intense desire to escape from the heat. It was regrettable that they missed one of the most thrilling episodes in the life of the Savior. If all the disciples went into the city, how did John know the details of a conversation he never heard? Is it possible that at a later date the Lord told His friend all that transpired on that unpleasant afternoon?

"There cometh a woman of Samaria to draw water: Jesus saith unto her, Give me to drink. . . . Then saith the woman of Samaria unto him, How is it that thou, being a Jew, askest drink of me, which am a woman of Samaria? for the Jews have no dealings with the Samaritans" (John 4:7, 9). The Samaritans were related to the Hebrews who were permitted to remain in the land when the rest of the population was taken to Babylon. They intermarried with pagans, and when the prisoners returned from captivity, animosity increased between the two parties. Samaritans believed that a sanctuary had been erected by Joshua on Mount Gerazim, and they accused the Jews of erecting an unauthorized temple in Jerusalem. Samaritans and Hebrews detested each other, and this fact made the woman ask, "How is it that thou, being a Jew, askest drink of me, which am a woman of Samaria? for the Jews have no dealings with the Samaritans."

The Lord responded by saying: "If thou knewest the gift of God, and who it is that saith to thee, Give me to drink; thou wouldest have asked of him, and he would have given thee living water" (John 4:10). That woman resembled modern people who have no conception of Christ's ability to supply spiritual refreshment. She was evidently astonished when He said, "Whosoever drinketh of this water shall thirst again: but whoso drinketh of the water that I shall give him, shall never thirst; but the water that I shall give him, shall be in him a well of living water springing up into everlasting life" (John 4:13–14). Yet, even then she did not comprehend the meaning of His statement. She replied, "Sir, give me this water, that I thirst not, neither come hither to draw" (John 4:15). Her eyes were only opened when she discovered He knew the secrets of her sinful life. When she testified to the other Samaritans she said, "Come, see a man which told me all things that ever I did: Is not this the Christ?" (John 4:29). Her influence on the townspeople was evident when they said: "Now we believe not because of thy saying; for we have heard him ourselves, and know that this is indeed the Christ, the Savior of the world" (John 4:42).

It was only then that the reason for Christ's visit to Sychar's well became evident. His mission had been accomplished; He never went there again. Evidently He saw the end from the beginning. He knew the immoral woman was not permitted to draw water at any other time, for to be seen in her company was an encouragement for gossip. Yet, when the salvation of many people was in question, no risk was too great to take. The Lord made a special effort to reach the well at midday.

The Distressed Woman . . . *Appreciating*

And it came to pass the day after, that he went into a city called Nain; and many of his disciples went with him, and much people. Now when he came nigh to the gate of the city, behold, there was a dead man carried out, the only son of his mother, and she was a widow; and much people of the city was with her (Luke 7:11–12).

Jesus only made one visit to Nain, and it is interesting to know He arrived at the right place at the precise moment when He was needed. Probably the mother whom He met was beyond tears. This was the second time she had been bereaved; she was a widow. Age, accident, or sickness had taken her husband. When the man died, her affection was lavished upon an only son. Alas, he also had been taken, and if his mother were like other people, she asked, "Why has God forsaken me?" There appeared to be no reason to continue her life, but the body had to be buried, and wearily, the mother began the journey to the graveside.

The procession was moving along at a normal speed until the pallbearers approached the gate of the city. There was much congestion, for many people of the community were present. Perhaps the family had been well known. Maybe the son had held some public office, and his death aroused sympathy throughout the city. The gateway was narrow, and an incoming crowd

141

impeded the progress of the procession. Men tried to move aside to allow the funeral to proceed, but there was not enough room for everybody. The tearful mother was anxious. Her son's body lay upon a plank-like frame which rested on the shoulders of men. The increasing crush from bystanders was distressing. The corpse might fall to the ground. Instinctively she clasped her hands, and then she saw the Stranger.

"And when the Lord saw her, he had compassion on her, and said unto her, Weep not. And he came and touched the bier: and they that bare him [the young man] stood still. And he said, Young man, I say unto thee, Arise. And he that was dead sat up, and began to speak. And he delivered him to his mother" (Luke 7:13–15). It was significant that on the day when Jesus visited Nain, He arrived at the precise moment when a funeral procession was passing through the gateway. Had the Lord been a minute later, the funeral would have been out of the city and on its way to the burial ground. Had the Savior been a minute earlier, He also would have been through the gate and proceeding on His way. He knew exactly what he was doing and arrived in time to help a distressed mother.

As far as is known, that was His only visit to Nain. "And he delivered him to his mother." The woman's arms were around her boy, but her eyes were focused on the Savior. Perhaps she never uttered a word, but her face said all that needed to be said. Words could not express the gratitude filling her soul. Until the end of time she would remember the Stranger whose eyes became pools of delight when He saw her grief being replaced by gladness. When she took her boy home the mother probably prepared a meal for him, but her thoughts were with the Savior. She had never met a man such as He. He was the chief among ten thousand, the altogether lovely one, who had come to the city to help her.

To conclude this study let it be repeated that Jesus went once to the following places: Tyre and Sidon, Sychar's Well, and the city of Nain. He earnestly desired to help three troubled women and refused to permit inconvenience to change His plans. This outstanding fact should help people know it is better to look for His arrival than to mourn His absence.

---

1. Ivor Powell, *Bible Cameos* (Grand Rapids: Kregel Publications, 1985), 91–92.

Pilate saith unto them, What shall I do then with Jesus which is called Christ? They all say unto him, Let him be crucified (Matthew 27:22).

The story has been told of a Native American and an Anglo man who attended the same evangelistic service. The Native American heard the Gospel and accepted the Savior immediately. The other man listened but went away convicted of his sin. Ultimately he also became a Christian, but when he met his friend, he asked, "How is it that you found peace quickly, while I was troubled for such a long time?" The Native American replied: "I tell you. A rich prince offered us new coats. You look at your nice suit, and decide it will last a little longer; I look at my blanket and decide it is no good. I accept the new coat, but you could not leave your old one. I go away happy; you stay sad in your suit." These conflicting attitudes may be seen in every walk of life, but nowhere can they be recognized as in the later stages of the life of Jesus of Nazareth.

Trying the Lord . . . *How Sinful*

Pilate saith unto them, What shall I do then with Jesus which is called Christ? They all say unto him, Let him be crucified. And the governor said, Why, what evil hath he done? But they cried out the more, saying, Let him be crucified. When Pilate saw that he could prevail nothing, but that rather a tumult was made, he took water, and washed his hands before the multitude, saying, I am innocent of the blood of this just person: see ye to it (Matt. 27:22–24).

The trial of Jesus was the most infamous in history, when all the principles of honesty and justice were violated. Pilate, the Roman judge, presided at an arraignment that was a farce. After questioning the Prisoner, he pronounced the Savior to be innocent and then permitted Him to be crucified. Through time and eternity Pilate will be remembered as a detestable man who thought more of himself than the honesty he was supposed to represent. Millions of people have recited his indictment saying: "I believe in God . . . and in His Son Jesus Christ . . . crucified under Pontius Pilate." Nothing will be able to remove the stain upon the record of that disappointing judge. Three irrefutable facts indicate his unworthiness.

He Suppressed Evidence

Jesus of Nazareth was not a stranger to public life. He had proved Himself to be the greatest benefactor known to mankind. For three years He had been the center of attraction, and unprecedented miracles transformed the life of many people. The blind had been made to see, lepers were cleansed, the lame walked, and even the dead were raised to life. His fame had spread throughout the land, and His exploits were discussed in every home and marketplace. Amazing kindness had been expressed in His words and deeds. The Savior denounced deception and hypocrisy, and was only opposed by people who were dominated by greed and hostility. False accusations had been made against Him, but when Pilate asked for evidence, none was forthcoming. When Jesus was delivered to His enemies, it was the equivalent of a modern judge allowing a lynch mob to murder an innocent victim.

He Ignored Conscience

When Pilate announced, "I find no fault in him," he admitted there was no blemish in the record of the accused. Why then did he refuse to release an innocent Man? Probably he feared the reactions of the political leaders. With the aid of a garrison of soldiers close at hand, any uprising could have been easily terminated, but critical reports sent to Caesar could undermine his authority and threaten his life. Solomon said: "The fear of man bringeth a snare: but whoso putteth his trust in the LORD shall be safe" (Prov. 29:25). Pilate would have been a wiser man had he accepted the advice given by the king of Israel.

He Rejected Advice

"When he (Pilate) was set down on the judgment seat, his wife sent unto him, saying, Have thou nothing to do with that just man: for I have suffered many things this day in a dream because of him" (Matt. 27:19). Even God Himself was concerned about the welfare of this unworthy man, for He suggested the special message sent by Pilate's spouse. Apparently the woman was greatly concerned about her husband. She knew he was presiding at the trial of Jesus of Nazareth and probably feared her partner might make the greatest mistake of his life. Her message represented God's final attempt to reach a lost soul. Actually, the woman wasted her time, for her partner was already sacrificing his soul!

Taunting the Lord . . . *How Senseless*

There were others who passed sentence upon the Savior, and their guilt was inexcusable.

> And Herod with his men of war set him [Jesus] at nought, and mocked him, and arrayed him in a gorgeous robe, and sent him again to Pilate (Luke 23:11).

> Likewise also the chief priests mocking said among themselves with the scribes, He saved others; himself he cannot save (Mark 15:31).

Their stupidity was expressed in scorn. Yet it was thought-provoking that they said, "He saved others." This fact was undeniable. There were many people able to speak of their healing, although they could not understand why He did not defend Himself. It would be interesting to know what the reactions of the high priest might have been had he become a leper. Would he have sought assistance from the Savior or allowed his disease to claim another victim? John wrote:

> And one of them, named Caiaphas, being the high priest that same year, said unto them, Ye know nothing at all, Nor consider that it is expedient for us, that one man should die for the people, and that the whole nation perish not. And this spake he not of himself: but being high priest that year, he prophesied that Jesus should die for that nation. And not for that nation only, but that also he should gather together in one the children of God that were scattered abroad (John 11:49–52).

"When the apostle John wrote his gospel a half century later, this utterance had assumed new importance. He believed an unseen Power had suggested the words to the mind of the prelate; that the voice of the Eternal Spirit had found expression in the words of Israel's leader. John saw in the prediction of the priest

145

the glorious fact that, through the death of Christ, other sheep would be brought together in the unity of a supreme fold, where one Shepherd would lead the flock. The statement: '*And not for that nation only*' is in perfect harmony with John 3:16 and 1 John 2:2."[1]

It remains mystifying how any sinful man could utter such sublime truth and still reject the Son of God. It remains clear that the final word rests with God and not man. Abraham Lincoln was correct when he said: "Better to remain silent and be thought a fool, than to speak and remove all doubt."

Troubling the Lord . . . *How Sad*

And when he was come near, he beheld the city, and wept over it, saying, If thou hadst known, even thou, at least in this thy day, the things which belong unto thy peace! but now they are hid from thine eyes. For the days shall come upon thee, that thine enemies shall cast a trench about thee, and compass thee around, and keep thee in on every side, And shall lay thee even with the ground, and thy children within thee; and they shall not leave in thee one stone upon another; because thou knewest not the time of thy visitation (Luke 19:41–44).

There are three references in the New Testament where Christ is reported to have shed tears. (1) He did so in Bethany where He saw how sin had hurt the world (John 11:35); (2) He wept over the city of Jerusalem when He predicted the doom of its inhabitants (Luke 19:41); and (3) He shed tears in the Garden of Gethsemane where sin was beginning to hurt Him (Heb. 5:7). His prediction concerning the fall of Jerusalem was literally fulfilled, for in the year 70 A.D. the city was totally destroyed, and even Christ was incapable of preventing the disaster. It remains an indisputable fact that even after the nation rejected Him, Christ continued to love the Jewish people. Nevertheless judgment becomes inevitable for unrepentant sinners. That fact should constitute a warning to all people. Even the love of the Savior is impotent when the righteousness of God is in question. Jesus knew these facts, but to watch as people lost their souls broke His heart. The Lord could not compel men to forsake their sinful ways, but one possibility remained. He took their sins to

146

the cross and suffered, the just for the unjust, in the hope He could bring sinners to God. The Scripture said: "Without shedding of blood is no remission" (Heb. 9:22). Apart from the cleansing power of the precious blood of Christ, pardon is an impossibility.

Trusting the Lord . . . *How Sublime*

And he [the thief] said unto Jesus, Lord, remember me when thou comest into thy kingdom. And Jesus said unto him, Verily I say unto thee, Today shalt thou be with me in paradise (Luke 23:42–43).

Now when the centurion saw what was done, he glorified God, saying, Certainly this was a righteous man (Luke 23:47).

And behold, there was a man named Joseph, a counselor; and he was a good man, and a just: (The same had not consented to the counsel and deed of them;) he was of Arimathaea, a city of the Jews: who also himself waited for the kingdom of God. This man went unto Pilate, and begged the body of Jesus (Luke 23:50–52).

The amazing influence of Jesus of Nazareth is something not easily understood. Conquerors dominate by military might, and the greater their armies, the more quickly their triumph comes. Enormous sums of money are necessary to sustain the effort, and taxes increase as the conflict continues. Jesus had no army and no weapons of war upon which to rely. His servants went forth armed openly with a desire to bring other people to their Master. From a small hill outside the city of Jerusalem ordinary men carried their message to the uttermost parts of the world and continued to tell their story until nations were compelled to listen. Jesus of Nazareth, the despised and rejected of men, became the King of Kings at whose feet millions of people bowed in reverence. He had no money except that which devoted followers supplied. He never wrote a book, and yet the libraries of the world are filled with volumes written about Him. It is almost beyond comprehension that the hands which were nailed to a cross now welcome all who labor and are heavy laden. It must be admitted that some people continue *to try*, *taunt,* and *trouble Him*, but happy are they who *trust* Him. It might be wise to ask to which class do we belong?

147

Dr. L. G. Broughton told the story of his going to preach in a fashionable church in an American city. At the end of his message he debated whether or not to issue an invitation, for he suspected such a procedure was unknown in that place. When he did, fourteen adults came forward to acknowledge their need of Christ. After the service, the wife of one of the church officers said, "I do not think that preacher should be allowed to disarrange the service for the sake of having a few people come to the front." The first man who responded to the invitation was a railway engineer who was killed in a wreck that Sunday evening. All people must decide what they will do with Jesus; but they should be in time!

1.   Ivor Powell, *John's Wonderful Gospel* (Grand Rapids: Kregel Publications, 1983), 249.

. . . Follow me. And he arose and followed him (Mark 2:14).

The difference between a hobo and a pilgrim is that the one person wanders, the other has a fixed destination. Life is a journey. The road may lead through green pastures or sandy deserts, but the end is assured. The path of life leads from the cradle to the grave. The Christian is a pilgrim who is always going somewhere. Five episodes of human history graphically display this fact.

The Call to Come

Two of every sort shall come unto thee, to keep them alive (Gen. 6:20).

Among the numerous criticisms of the biblical account of the flood is the statement that it would have been impossible for Noah to collect two of every kind of animal upon the earth. One cynic wrote: "It would have been necessary for Noah to live six hundred lifetimes—not six hundred years—to accomplish that task." Evidently the critic was not a careful student of the Scripture. The patriarch was never asked to collect animals. He was told "two of every sort shall come unto thee." Noah's responsibility was the completion of the ark; it was the work of the Lord to bring the species destined to repopulate the world. That, to some degree, was the greatest achievement since the creation of the world. Animals that enjoyed the company of their kind, that thrived on the grass God had grown, suddenly became discontented and restless. The pasture which had been enjoyable failed to please, and the company of other animals became boring. A strange agitation began to destroy the tranquility of the animals. They appeared to be hearing a voice that said, "Leave it, leave it." Jehovah had chosen two of every kind of beast; the others were content to stay where they were. They came from all directions and presented a sight never before seen. Giraffes and rabbits, elephants and field mice walked side by side. They all appeared to be aware of the need to get into the ship that Noah had completed. If it were possible for animals to talk, the rabbit might have looked at the stately giraffe to say, "With a neck like that, you should be safe anywhere." The mice might have said to the lions and elephants, "We understand why we need help, but you are strong." Perhaps they might have replied, "Little fellows, it is not *what* we are that matters but *where* we are! The smallest inside that ship will be safe; the strongest outside will be lost. Come on, get in before the door closes."

That picture from an ancient world suggests that Jesus knew what He was saying when He uttered the words: "But as the days of Noah were, so shall also the coming of the Son of man be" (Matt. 24:37). As it was, so shall it be. God was and is still determined to populate the new world with those He will call. When the Holy Spirit moves upon the consciences of men and women, worldly pleasure ceases to satisfy, and the company of the unredeemed is no longer attractive. Then God's voice suggests the need to search for safety. The universal church of Jesus Christ supplies evidence that those who have heard His call have come from every tongue and nation to find refuge within His ark of salvation. What we may be is of no importance; *where we are* is all that matters. Jesus said: "Verily, verily, I say unto you. He that heareth my word, and believeth on him that sent me, hath everlasting life, and shall not come into condemnation; but is passed from death unto life" (John 5:24). The first pilgrimage leads to the Cross of Calvary.

The Call to Leave

"And the LORD went before them by day in a pillar of a cloud, to lead them the way; and by night in a pillar of fire, to give them light; to go by day and night" (Exod. 13:21).

The Lord brought the animals into the ark because He intended to take them into a new world. When Jehovah redeemed Israel in Egypt, it became evident He was determined to lead His people into Canaan.

The ancient Hebrews were inexperienced in war. They had no weapons with which to defend themselves, and only a miracle of divine intervention could guarantee their survival in the wilderness. Without the presence of God extinction would have been inevitable. It became increasingly evident that the safety of the nation depended on the fact that Jehovah remained in the midst of His people. Israel would never be alone. The cloud which hovered over the tabernacle by day and the pillar of fire which led through the night assured them the Lord would be a Helper in time of trouble. With His assistance they could accomplish the impossible.

During the journey to Canaan God lived among His people; today He lives within His people. When Paul wrote to the Corinthian church he said, "Know ye not that ye are the temple of God, and that the Spirit of God dwelleth in you?" (1 Cor. 3:16). It is an amazing fact that throughout the world the Holy Spirit guides God's children. His leadership is available for the African in his jungle hut, the mysterious Chinese believer in his distant country, and to all nations of the world. The cloud by day and the pillar of fire by night may still be seen by those whose faith sees the invisible. God continues to lead His people, and the end of the pilgrimage is assured. "But the path of the just is as the shining light, that shineth more and more unto the perfect day" (Prov. 4:18). "In my Father's house are many mansions: if it were not so, I would have told you. I go to prepare a place for you. And if I go and prepare a place for you, I will come again, and receive you unto myself; that where I am, there may ye be also" (John 14:2–3). The redeemed of the Lord were never meant to remain in Egypt!

The Call to Follow

"Wherefore he saith, When he ascended up on high, he led captivity captive, and gave gifts unto men. (Now that he ascended, what is it but that he also descended first into the lower parts of the earth? He that descended is the same also that ascended up far above all heavens, that he might fill all things)" (Eph. 4:8–10).

Between the death and resurrection of the Savior, He performed a special mission—to open a door and proclaim freedom to multitudes of saints who had been unable to enter into the presence of God. When Simon Peter preached on the Day of Pentecost, he made an important statement: "For David is not ascended into the heavens" (Acts 2:34). The sins of the world had not yet been abolished, and, consequently, the people who had died—both saints and sinners—went to a place called Sheol, or Hades (see Luke 16:19–31). The death of Christ made it possible for the Savior to liberate His people and lead them into

151

the presence of His Father. He appeared before millions of Old Testament saints to say: "It is time to leave. Follow me." The gates of Sheol were opened, and one of the greatest parades commenced. One-half of Sheol remained occupied by the unrighteous people awaiting judgment, but the other half was emptied as the Lord led multitudes into the presence of the Almighty. Language is too impoverished to describe the joy of the released souls; they beheld the Savior and knew His redeeming death had made their homegoing possible. When they heard Christ saying, "Brethren, it is time to leave. Follow me," they were ready to commence their journey.

The Call to Ascend

For the Lord himself shall descend from heaven with a shout with the voice of the archangel, and with the trump of God: and the dead in Christ shall rise first. Then we which are alive and remain shall be caught up together with them in the clouds, to meet the Lord in the air: and so shall we ever be with the Lord (1 Thess. 4:16–17).

When the Lord liberated the ancient saints, He led them by a new and living way into the presence of His Father. Throughout the Old Testament period believers had gone to the righteous section of Sheol, but that never happened again. When saints die they go immediately into the presence of God. "We are confident, I say, and willing rather to be absent from the body, and to be present with the Lord" (2 Cor. 5:8).

Bodies are not essential for survival in the presence of God. Nevertheless, it is said that "we shall have a body like unto his glorious body" (Phil. 3:21). Without them it would be impossible for the church to reign with Christ on earth. The mortal body must put on immortality, and the corruptible must be superseded by incorruption. This exciting transformation will take place when the Savior returns for His Bride—the church. When the trumpet of the archangel announces the return of Christ, the bodies of saints will be raised to newness of life and caught up into the clouds where they will be claimed by their former owners. Resurrected bodies will hear and answer the call of God, and the Rapture of the church will present one of the most glittering spectacles ever witnessed. Redeemed souls who have died will respond to the summons of the Almighty, and the heavens will be filled with people resplendent in immortality. Angels will watch in surpassing wonder, and the sky will resound with the song: "Worthy is the Lamb who was slain to redeem us by His blood." Thereafter God's kingdom will be filled with excitement as preparation is made for the marriage of the Son of God.

The Call to Return

> And I saw heaven opened, and behold a white horse; and he that sat upon him was called Faithful and True, and in righteousness he doth judge and make war. His eyes were as a flame of fire, and on his head were many crowns; and he hath a name written, that no man knew, but he himself. . . . And the armies which were in heaven followed him upon white horses, clothed in fine linen, white and clean. . . . And he hath on his vesture and on his thigh a name written, KING OF KINGS AND LORD OF LORDS (Rev. 19:11–16).

God intends to purify the world. Through His servant Isaiah He said: "The wolf also shall dwell with the lamb, and the leopard shall lie down with the kid; and the calf and the young lion and the fatling together; and a little child shall lead them. And the cow and the bear shall feed; their young ones shall lie down together: and the lion shall eat straw like an ox. And the suckling child shall play on the hole of the asp, and the weaned child shall put his hand on the cockatrice' den. They shall not hurt nor destroy in all my holy mountain: for the earth shall be full of the knowledge of the Lord, as the waters cover the sea" (Isa. 11:6–8). God intends to make this planet what it was originally meant to be.

This was to be the introduction of God's final attempt to purify the earth. Later legions of human beings deceived by Satan would make an attempt to destroy the followers of God, but their efforts would be destroyed by fire descending from heaven (Rev. 20:7–10). That the saints will accompany their Lord on this final episode suggests questions difficult to answer. They are described as riding upon white horses. Does that mean that heaven has vast stables of purebred horses? That arrangement would require innumerable hostlers to attend to the constant needs of the animals. If that were true, it might be difficult to appreciate many implications. Was John using terms easily understood on earth to express the omnipotence of the Lord? The saints will share in that tremendous parade which will bring them back to earth. Paul was so convinced of the continuity of fellowship between Christ and His followers, that he wrote to the Romans saying: "For I am persuaded, that neither death, nor life, nor angels, nor principalities, nor powers, nor things present, nor things to come, Nor height, nor depth, nor any other creature, shall be able to separate us from the love of God, which is in Christ Jesus our Lord" (Rom. 8:38–39). God is able to complete what He commences. The parades mentioned in this study endorse that fact.

And he departed, and began to publish in Decapolis how great things Jesus had done for him: and all men did marvel (Mark 5:20).

. . . go thy way, shew thyself to the priest, and offer for thy cleansing those things which moses commanded, for a testimony unto them. But he went out, and began to publish it much, and to blaze abroad the matter . . . and they came to him from every quarter (Mark 1:44–45).

The woman then left her waterpot, and went her way into the city, and saith to the men, Come, see a man, which told me all things that ever I did: is not this the Christ (John 4:28–29)?

Therefore they that were scattered abroad went every where preaching the word (Acts 8:4).

Evangelism is the spearhead of the church's attack on sin. It is the secret of every advance made in the name of the Savior. Throughout the history of the church, God has sent gifted people to assist in the propagation of the Gospel. These preachers possessed special insight into the Scriptures and an undying passion to win men and women for Christ. Peter and Paul were the first of a long line of successors whose chief interest in life was winning lost people. The message delivered on the Day of Pentecost established and strengthened the church, for thousands of Jews accepted Jesus as the Messiah. The first assembly was established, and later the apostle told the people in Ephesus that special gifts had been bestowed upon certain folk. "He gave some, apostles; and some, prophets; and some, evangelists; and some, pastors and teachers" (Eph. 4:11). These talents enabled the early church to extend its ministry throughout the world. Peter was the evangelist at Pentecost, but he was followed by Paul whose missionary journeys took him throughout the Roman Empire. Every age has had its brilliant preachers, and Luther, Whitfield, Wesley, Finney, and others of their kind influenced multitudes of people. To that list Billy Graham and other modern preachers can now be added. The world has been enriched because of their ministry.

155

It must never be forgotten that however wonderful these preachers were, they did not reveal the true secret of New Testament evangelism. The greatest outpouring of God's blessing became evident when the thousands of converts, influenced by Simon Peter, returned to their homes in other lands to explain what had transformed their lives. Great and famous speakers are always an asset, but they cannot compare with the impact made by individuals who tell friends of the risen Christ. When each member of a church becomes an evangelist, that assembly becomes an institution against which even the gates of hell cannot prevail. Four outstanding occasions mentioned in the Scriptures invite investigation. They supply an example which every Christian should follow.

Commissioned by Christ . . . *How Suggestive*

And when he was come into the ship, he that had been possessed with the devil, prayed him that he might be with him. Howbeit, Jesus suffered him not, but saith unto him, Go home to thy friends, and tell them how great things the Lord hath done for thee, and hath had compassion on thee. And he departed and began to publish in Decapolis how great things Jesus had done for him: and all men did marvel (Mark 5:18–20).

The irate hog farmers of Gadara had made their choice; they had asked Jesus to leave the district. One of the men had lost two thousand swine, and neighbors feared a similar loss. They had no basic animosity against the Lord, and would have given Him a great welcome if He had not interfered with their business. The men had worked long and hard to establish herds of swine, but within minutes Jesus had destroyed their efforts. They appreciated the deliverance of the demoniac, but not even his transformation could compensate for their loss. If the Visitor were allowed to continue, they would be bankrupt! The sooner He left, the better it would be for all concerned. "And they began to pray him to depart out of their coasts" (Mark 5:17).

The former demoniac watched the proceedings and asked if he could join the company, but Jesus replied, "Son, I have a better idea. I would love to take you, but you can be of more value here. Your neighbors have asked me to leave; they believe it will cost too much if I stay. They will not hear me, but you live here. They will listen to your testimony. Go home to thy friends and tell them what happened. Tell them about Me." The Lord only asked him to tell his friends, but the man quickly found a much larger congregation. "And he departed and began to publish in Decapolis how great things Jesus had done for him: *and all men did marvel*" (Mark 5:20).

There is no record that Jesus ever returned to Gadara, but since Palestine was a small country, people did not have to travel great distances to hear the Savior. Great crowds came to Christ, and perhaps many of those hearers were first inspired by the testimony of the demoniac. The Savior wanted His convert to inform others of his deliverance. He also depends upon us to tell others He remains unchanged.

Cautioned by Christ . . . *How Strange*

And there came a leper to him. . . . And Jesus, moved with compassion, put forth his hand, and touched him. . . . And as soon as he had spoken, the leprosy departed from him, and he was cleansed. And he straitly charged him, and forthwith sent him away; And saith unto him, See thou say nothing to any man. . . . But he went out, and began to publish it much, and to blaze abroad the matter, insomuch that Jesus could no more openly enter into the city, but was without in desert places; and they came to him from every quarter (Mark 1:40–45).

According to the Levitical law, a leper who believed he had been cleansed was required to present himself before the priest for an official examination. Real leprosy was incurable, but some of the other skin diseases could be cured. When this took place, official recognition had to be obtained before the leper was permitted to rejoin society. Certain offerings had to be made, and it was for this reason Jesus commanded the man to "offer for thy cleansing those things which Moses commanded, for a testimony unto them" (Mark 1:44). Unless the man did as he was required, he could be arrested by the authorities. Jesus was careful to remind the man of his duty. In addition, his testimony would carry the good news to priests who might otherwise never hear it. The cleansing of the leper was certain to cause great excitement. Thousands of people crowding narrow streets could bring

157

danger to individuals and anger the authorities. Therefore, the Master wisely commanded the man to remain silent. That the man disobeyed brings mixed emotions to our hearts. The leper's disobedience made it necessary for the Lord to retire into the desert. His enthusiastic testimony hindered other sufferers who might have found it difficult to travel. There are times when enthusiasm runs away with brains! Happy and wise are they who know when to speak and when to say nothing.[1] Enthusiasm is a fire within the soul. When it is controlled, it supplies warmth, comfort, and energy. When it is not, it becomes one of the most destructive forces known to man.

Captivated by Christ . . . *How Surprising*

> The woman then left her waterpot, and went her way into the city, and saith to the men, Come, see a man which told me all things that ever I did: is not this the Christ? (John 4:28–29).

When the Savior was upon earth, women did not enjoy the privileges known in the modern world. Samaritan wives were little more than slaves, and those of ill-repute were avoided by almost everybody. The woman of Samaria had a terrible reputation, and every decent citizen detested her company. She had been married five times and finally consented to live with another man. It was not revealed what happened to the five husbands. They either died or decided they would be happier apart from the woman who had an insatiable appetite for male companions. Either she was compelled by law to draw water at midday or had discovered it was better to obtain supplies when spiteful people were absent.

She was now causing a disturbance in the streets of Sychar. Even the self-righteous were attracted, for many people were present, and there was safety in numbers! Her voice was loud, her excitement intense. She had met an extraordinary man who had revealed closely guarded secrets. How could He do this if He were not the Messiah? She said, "Come, see a man which told me all things that ever I did. Is not this the Christ?" Her forthright testimony, glowing face, and evident sincerity aroused the curiosity of the listeners. They went to see the strange Man and later confessed: "Now we believe, not because of thy saying: for we have heard him ourselves, and know that this is indeed the Christ, the Savior of the world" (John 4:42).

That woman became the first female evangelist. Her testimony helped to convince an entire community that Jesus was the Messiah. Every Christian knows the story of Christ's visit to the well at Sychar, but many fail to emulate the example set by the woman whom He met there. Her shameful past was forgotten, and oblivious to the fact that some of her neighbors would criticize her actions, she was compelled to tell others about the Savior. Her testimony influenced the community, but that was not her primary concern. The way God used her testimony was amazing. The question might be asked, "What would be accomplished if He had the assistance of a thousand others of her type?" Innumerable church members seldom speak about the Lord in the marketplace, the office, or even among friends. It is easy to sing: "I've a story to tell to the nations," but it is just as necessary to deliver the same message to the people we meet every day.

Captivated by Christ... *How Superb*

As for Saul, he made havock of the church, entering into every house, and haling men and women committed them to prison. Therefore they that were scattered abroad, went everywhere preaching the word (Acts 8:3–4).

It should be easier for Christians to speak of Christ's power to save than to converse about politics, the weather, or sporting events. Certain people respect and honor vows of silence, but that should never apply to anyone whose heart yearns to tell the message of Christ. Every believer in the Savior is commissioned to become a witness, and that duty is clearly defined. When fierce persecution made it impossible to remain in one place, the early Christians sought shelter in other cities. When they were driven even further, they continued to speak of the Lord, and everywhere churches were formed, people saved, and the kingdom of God extended.

You Are My Grandfather!

He was one of the few who ever succeeded in startling me! He had rushed up a long staircase, taking the steps two or three at a time. His round face glowed attractively, and his eyes danced with merriment. He shot out a hand and asked, "Aren't you Ivor Powell?" Rather warily I informed him that his deductions were correct. I was at his service. What could I do for him? His face immediately crinkled, and his eyes became even more mischievous as he half shouted, "I'm glad to meet you. You are my grandfather." He shook my hand as if it had been a pump handle, and, while the up-and-down motions continued, I steadily gazed into his eyes and wondered how long he had been ill! He enjoyed my bewilderment. "Yes, it's true. You are my grandfather. Pleased to meet you, sir!" By this time I was capable of expecting anything. If this were one of my grandchildren, he would surely explain the miracle, since I had no children! And having overcome that obstacle, he would undoubtedly tell me of his financial difficulties and ask his benevolent relative to have pity on the rising generation! I therefore waited for the worst. His words were like a torrent suddenly released from a dam. Sparkling, scintillating, entrancing, they tumbled over red walls and refreshed my waiting soul. "Mr. Powell, do you remember a fish and chip shop in Honiton, Devonshire? Do you remember going into the back of the place to lead the assistant to Christ? Well, sir, he won me for the Savior. He's my father in the faith. See? And you led him to Christ, so you must be my grandfather. Glad to meet you. Sorry I can't stop. God bless you." He turned and fled down the stairway as if he were being chased by a thousand Philistines.

A fish and chip shop in Honiton, Devonshire! Yes, I remembered it quite well. The Pilgrim Preachers toured Devonshire in the summer of 1931, and at that time I was the junior member of the party. Twelve months earlier Mr. Ernest Luff had invited me to join "his boys," and thus had commenced one of the most delightful phases of my life. We did not have many friends in Honiton, but someone gave us the use of a schoolroom in which to sleep. We had to supply our own food, and thus after every evening service I went in search of that national asset for the hungry—the fish and chip shop.

There were several people waiting for the fresh cooking french fries, so I took my place in the line. The proprietor was a happy type of fellow. He talked incessantly to his customers, and they seemed to like him. An unmistakable shine was upon his face, and in true layman fashion I debated the cause of the glow. Homiletically there were three possibilities—chip-fat, hair-oil, or radiance emanating from within. Of course, my thoughts were stupid, but at least they helped to pass the time, for those chips were a long time cooking. Then quite suddenly a whisper suggested that I should seek the cause of the man's shining face. I was truly staggered, for such actions would savor of lunacy. I dismissed the idea as outrageous. But the whisper would not be silenced. When he looked inquiringly at me, I gave him my order, and then added, "I like the shine on your face. You look like a happy Christian!" Immediately he turned around, and the glow intensified. "I *am* a Christian, and I'm very happy, thank God. Are you a Christian?" I assured him that such was the case. Then he asked where I belonged, and what I was doing. When I supplied the necessary information, he answered, "Young man, I'm glad you came in tonight. My assistant, who is cutting chips, is concerned about his soul, and I'm unable to help him. Perhaps God sent you to lead him to Christ. Will you try?" He told his assistant that I wished to speak with him, and there in the back room of the premises I led the boy to the Savior. Later, when I wanted to pay for my supper, the boss grinned and said something about the laborer being worthy of his hire. That was the only occasion in my life when the reward for preaching was given in fish and french fries! I have never met those fellows since that night, but the "grandchild" appearing at the top of the London staircase more than confirmed the fact that the babe in Christ has grown to manhood.[2]

1. Ivor Powell, *Mark's Superb Gospel* (Grand Rapids: Kregel Publications, 1985), 41.

2. Ivor Powell, *Bible Windows* (Grand Rapids: Kregel Publications, 1985), 79.

THE IMPORTANCE OF A POSITIVE NEGATIVE

He ... shall not come into condemnation (John 5:24).

Dr. F. E. Marsh, who was one of the most brilliant preachers in Britain, spoke of a minister who visited an elderly but despondent member of his congregation. She was very concerned about the possibility of financial insecurity, and said, "I fear I shall be in want." He listened to her problems and then began to read Psalm 23. "The Lord is my shepherd; I shall want." "No, no," she cried, "It's not like that in my Bible." He read it again making the same mistake. Again she objected, and taking the book from his hand, read, "The Lord is my shepherd; I shall *not* want." "There," she cried again, "I told you it was not like that in my Bible." Then, quite suddenly, she realized the mistake had been made to draw attention to her lack of faith. To her credit it can be said she never repeated her mistake. The word—*not*—seems insignificant and unimportant, but when it is removed from certain Scriptures, the biblical spectrum changes.

The Possible Peace

Verily, verily, I say unto you, He that heareth my word, and believeth on him that sent me, hath everlasting life, and shall *not* come into condemnation; but is passed from death unto life (John 5:24).

One of the saddest experiences in life is to meet a fellow Christian who lives in constant fear of being rejected by God. The lack of assurance is appalling, for it keeps the soul in a state of uncertainty and ruins the joy of salvation.

When I was a young Christian in a Welsh church, one of the leaders often said he hoped to be accepted by the Lord and confessed he feared the possibility of rejection. In fairness to the man, let it be admitted he had made profession of faith, but the promising beginning had been followed by serious backsliding. He feared this might happen again and said he could not believe God would forgive a repeated mistake. His viewpoint troubled me. The brother was always looking at himself. I believe he would have welcomed a premature death to avoid the possibility of future failure. I was reluctant to argue with him, but my childlike faith in the

162

promises of Christ made it impossible for me to agree with him. I had already discovered that Christ said to His disciples that those who belong to Him have "everlasting life and shall *not* come into condemnation." Remove the *not* from the promise, and the entire fabric of Christianity begins to disintegrate. Men are not saved from the penalty of sin because of their unbroken loyalty to the Lord. They are accepted because the Savior bore their sin, paid their debt, and guaranteed they would never perish. Either He meant what He said, or He was untruthful. It is regrettable when a Christian becomes unfaithful, but even that cannot break the bonds that bind him to Christ. It is wiser to trust in the Lord than to worry about things that may never happen.

The Possessed Power

Neither yield ye your members as instruments of unrighteousness unto sin: but yield yourselves unto God, as those that are alive from the dead, and your members as instruments of righteousness unto God. For sin shall *not* have dominion over you: for ye are not under the law, but under grace (Rom. 6:13–14).

Paul wrote to the Christians in Rome, saying, "For whom he did foreknow, he also did predestinate to be conformed to the image of his Son, that he might be the firstborn among many brethren" (Rom. 8:29). It might be true to say that God is far more concerned with what we are going to be than with what we were! He has saved us from the uttermost, but the miracle of grace will never be completed until Christians have been changed into the likeness of the Savior. It has often been said that although the Lord brought Israel out of Egypt in one night, it took Him forty years to bring Egypt out of Israel. Unfortunately, the journey through life is hindered by enemies, many of whom live within the believer. It is often easier and wiser to confront external difficulties than to subdue carnal inclinations of self. Even Paul said: "O wretched man that I am! who shall deliver me from the body of this death!" (Rom. 7:24). It was evident even to the Lord that man was unequal to the task of conquering himself. Therefore, it was arranged that God's strength should be made perfect in our weakness—the Holy Spirit came to reside within the believer to become the Commander-in-Chief in the ongoing struggles against evil. To fight alone could only lead to defeat. To assist the Lord

163

and follow His guidance makes possible the realization of the promise: "Sin shall not have dominion over you." The secret of continuing victory over self, sin, and Satan is found in the apostle's command: "Yield yourselves unto God." When General Booth, the founder of the Salvation Army, was asked what was the secret of the continuing success of the movement, he replied, "God has had all there was of me." That was, and still is, the secret of successful service for the Savior. Paul said, "Not I, but Christ."

The Permanent Pleasure

> But one thing is needful: and Mary hath chosen that good part, which shall *not* be taken away from her (Luke 10:42).

What happened in Bethany two thousand years ago has been immortalized within the hearts of Christians everywhere. Martha's irritability regarding her sister's avoiding work in the kitchen and the Lord's intervention in the dispute is known throughout the world. Mary was so intent on sitting at the feet of Jesus, that all thought about preparing a meal was forgotten.

> And she [Martha] had a sister called Mary, which also sat at Jesus' feet, and heard his word. But Martha was cumbered about much serving, and came to him, and said, Lord, dost thou not care that my sister hath left me to serve alone? Bid her therefore that she help me. And Jesus answered and said unto her, Martha, Martha, thou art careful and troubled about many things: But one thing is needful: and Mary hath chosen that good part, which shall not be taken away from her (Luke 10:39–42).

To change the reading to "the good part which shall be taken away from her," would not only spoil the story, it would offend the conscience of Christians in every nation. Evidently the Savior loved a gracious listener. He ministered to needs within Mary's soul. When she sat at His feet, she believed she was in the presence of God. All housewives appreciate the frustration of Martha and understand why she became annoyed. Nevertheless, when Jesus compared the sincere work of the one woman with the glowing devotion of her sister, He judged between the two and said: "Mary hath chosen the good part, which shall *not* be taken away from her." Service is necessary and wonderful, but adoration and worship are better. Christians should seek that privilege and refuse to allow its glories to be lost. The Savior no longer appears before His followers, but the Holy Spirit has taken His place. His word can still be heard; blessed are they who spend time with their Bible.

The Promised Presence

> I will never leave thee, nor forsake thee. So that we may boldly say, The Lord is my helper, and I will *not* fear what man shall do unto me (Heb. 13:5–6).

When Moses died, it became the privilege and responsibility of Joshua to continue the work which the patriarch had commenced. This was a task that wise men would have avoided. The tribes of Israel were cynical and rebellious. They did not hesitate to criticize Moses, and it was to be expected their attitude would remain unchanged. Joshua agreed to become the leader of the nation only because he was assured this was the will of God for his life. His success was sustained by his faith in the promises of Jehovah. Realizing he would not find sufficient strength in his own capabilities, he relied upon the everlasting arms of God's kindness and remembered the promises given to him.

> There shall not any man be able to stand before thee all the days of thy life: as I was with Moses, so I will be with thee: I will not fail thee, nor farsake thee. Be strong and of a good courage: for unto this people shalt thou divide for an inheritance the land, which I sware unto their fathers to give them. Only be thou strong and very courageous, that thou mayest observe to do according to all the law, which Moses my servant commanded thee: turn not from it to the right hand or to the left, that thou mayest prosper whithersoever thou goest. This book of the law shall not depart out of thy mouth; but thou shalt meditate therein day and night, that thou mayest observe to do according to all that is written therein: for then thou shalt make thy way propsperous, and then thou shalt have good success (Josh. 1:5–8).

The entire nation knew that God had been with Moses, and the new leader believed the presence of God would be just as

165

real to him. This promise was amplified when God's special messenger arrived. "And it came to pass, when Joshua was by Jericho, that he lifted up his eyes and looked, and, behold, there stood a man over against him with his sword drawn in his hand: and Joshua went unto him, and said unto him, Art thou for us, or for our adversaries? And he said, Nay; but as captain of the host of the Lord am I now come. . . . Loose thy shoe from off thy foot; for the place whereon thou standest is holy. And Joshua did so" (Josh. 5:13–15). Thus was the leader of the tribes assured he was never alone. Somewhere nearby stood the Lord who was aware of everything that was happening.

The same assurance filled the mind of the early church leaders. The writer to the Hebrews reminded his readers that God promised never to leave His people.

The Prolonged Prosperity

A bruised reed shall he not break, and the smoking flax shall he not quench: he shall bring forth judgment unto truth. He shall *not* fail nor be discouraged, till he hath set judgment in the earth: and the isles shall wait for his law (Isa. 42:3–5).

Isaiah provided many entrancing word pictures, but this was one of his best. It must be remembered that authors used reeds as pens, and when through excessive use the end of the reed became saturated, it was replaced by a new one. Similarly, flax was used in primitive lamps, and when the wick or flax became old, it was removed. Perhaps Isaiah was actually doing one of these chores when God whispered, "When my servant comes, he will not abandon nor discard an old friend; He will breathe upon the flax and rejuvenate its flame." This renewing ministry will continue until "he has set judgment in the earth, and the isles wait for his law." This was a special covenant made with the Savior, but it applies to all who, following in their Master's footsteps, endeavor to be Christlike. David was elderly when he wrote, "I have been young, and now am old; yet have I not seen the righteous forsaken, nor his seed begging bread" (Ps. 37:25). The Lord reiterated that promise when He said, "But seek ye first the kingdom of God, and his righteousness; and all these things shall be added unto you" (Matt. 6:33). He also said, "Give, and it shall be given you; good measure, pressed down, and

166

shaken together, and running over, shall men give into your bosom. For with the same measure that ye mete withal it shall be measured to you again" (Luke 6:38). It is impossible to outgive the Giver of every good and perfect gift. God is never a debtor—He is more generous than any of His people.

But Thomas, one of the twelve, called Didymus, was not with them when Jesus came. The other disciples therefore said unto him, We have seen the Lord. But he said unto them, Except I shall see in his hands the print of the nails, and put my finger into the print of the nails, and thrust my hand into his side, I will not believe (John 20:24–25).

It is unfortunate that mistakes are remembered much longer than achievements. A man may devote a lifetime to meritorious service, but one mistake can ruin his reputation. He will be remembered not for his wonderful deeds, but for the blot on his record. Probably, Thomas is the most outstanding example of that regrettable fact. The designation "Doubting Thomas" has become an integral part of language; even people who never read the Bible use it. Anyone who exhibits lack of faith, confidence, and trust or fears the future, is said to be "A Doubting Thomas." Even atheists refer to the Scriptures when they use the words regarding Thomas. It is to be regretted that the finer qualities of a man's character may be obscured by an isolated flaw. This is unfortunate, for the disciple of Jesus was a fine man whose actions were above reproach. Many of the qualities he exhibited would increase the effectiveness of any Christian.

Thomas the Courageous . . . *How Stimulating*

Thomas was also called Didymus, which means a twin. Many have speculated concerning this, but the most likely interpretation is that he had a twin brother or sister. Perhaps he was the only one to survive. Others have suggested that the Lord gave the name to His disciple to indicate the man could be elated one moment, and dejected the next. He was a mixture of faith and fear. It is wise to remember that the Savior knew this even before He invited the man to become a disciple, but in spite of the imperfections Jesus wanted Thomas to become His follower. Jesus never sought perfect people. He called folk who were filled with flaws, and that should encourage everybody.

168

Then after that saith he to his disciples, Let us go into Judaea again. His disciples say unto him, Master, the Jews of late sought to stone thee, and goest thou thither again? . . . Then said Thomas, which is called Didymus, unto his fellow disciples, Let us also go, that we may die with him (John 11:7–8, 16).

Evidently Thomas had reached a conclusion. Life without the Lord would be empty and meaningless. It would be better to die with Him than to live without Him. If, as had been suggested, the Jews stoned Jesus, death would be brutally painful, yet to Thomas, even that was preferable to living without the Master. The New Testament describes people who deserted Christ because to follow Him would mean sacrifice and loss. The rich young ruler refused to become a disciple because the cost appeared to be too great. Thomas saw only the emptiness of a life deprived of fellowship with Jesus. Maybe the man was pessimistic and morbid, but although he sincerely believed martyrdom was approaching, he found consolation in the fact that he would be with Christ in death as he had been in life. Thomas should be a shining example to every Christian, but unfortunately there are many people who are not so dedicated. They applaud miracles but dislike hardship.

Thomas the Candid . . . *How Surprising*

And if I go and prepare a place for you, I will come again and receive you unto myself; that where I am, there ye may be also. And whither I go ye know, and the way ye know. Thomas saith unto him, Lord, we know not whither thou goest; and how can we know the way? Jesus saith unto him, I am the way, the truth, and the life: no man cometh unto the Father, but by me (John 14:3–6).

Preconceived ideas are often a menace. It is difficult to persuade anyone who has already formulated an opinion. The disciples followed Jesus because they believed Him to be the Messiah. When they saw His miracles, they smiled and imagined what would happen when He became king. They expected Him to expel the Romans and establish within Palestine the eternal kingdom of God. Yet as time passed, they became confused and bewildered. The Lord disliked violence of any kind, so how could He overcome invaders? Romans would never withdraw willingly. When Jesus urged listeners to love their enemies and do good to obnoxious people, those disturbed men hardly knew what to think. They looked for a kingdom which would surpass in excellence the empire of Solomon, yet Jesus seemed to be vague and mysterious when He spoke of building mansions for His followers. Where and when would He do this? Where would He obtain the necessary materials to complete the project? How long would it take to finish the job? Then to make matters worse, Jesus predicted His approaching death. How could He complete anything if He were dead? Their Master's actions were difficult to understand.

Jesus could expel demons, heal the sick, and calm stormy seas. On the other hand, He could be so tired that even the noises of a raging storm could not disturb His slumber. It was not a cause for amazement when the disciples failed to comprehend the things he said and did. All of them were troubled, but only Thomas expressed concern. Finally, he could not remain silent and seemed to say, "Lord, You speak of many mansions to be built somewhere, yet here You have no place to lay your head. You are going somewhere, and we are expected to know where. Lord, the time has come to be explicit. Tell us plainly what you are planning to do, for we all seem to be going around in circles. Explain what is on your mind, and we shall have a better chance to cooperate. 'We know not whither thou goest; and how can we know the way?'" (John 14:5).

Any one of the twelve could have spoken similar words, but no one did. Thomas alone expressed his problem, and for that he should be congratulated. A man who knows everything has lived too long, and he who never asks questions has an undeveloped brain.

Thomas the Critical . . . *How Stubborn*

But Thomas, one of the twelve, called Didymus, was not with them when Jesus came (John 20:24).

Where was he? Why had Thomas, temporarily at least, left his brethren? As far as the disciples were concerned, they were in enemy territory where merciless foes had crucified their Master. Apart from the large upper room in Jerusalem, they had no place in which to hide and no friend to offer shelter. Yet Thomas

170

had gone somewhere! Possibly he could no longer appreciate morbid companions. Filled with joyful anticipation they had watched their Lord riding majestically into the city of David and had heard the welcoming cheers from crowds which lined the streets. Then treachery overwhelmed them, and their world fell apart. Language could not express the misery that filled their souls, and when Simon Peter suggested a return to fishing, the others knew there was little else to be done. Even in his better moments Thomas was prone to be somber and depressed, but on that particular day he probably wished he had died with his Master. Opening the door, Thomas went out to be somewhere, anywhere. But where could he go? Maybe he wandered around the streets or sat on a bench, but the end result was never in doubt. He returned whence he had come. When he entered the room, he stopped and stared. The gloom that had troubled his colleagues had disappeared; the disciples were happy and smiling. Some might even have been whistling a merry tune. Were they crazy? Had grief affected their sanity?

> The other disciples therefore said unto him, We have seen the Lord. But he said unto them, Except I shall see in his hands the print of the nails, and put my finger into the print of the nails, and thrust my hand into his side, I will not believe (John 20:25).

"I will not believe." Thomas was a little belligerent. His eyes revealed indignation. The brethren had taken leave of their senses! He would have to see the nail prints in the Lord's hands before he could believe their absurd statements. His fingertips would have to explore the wounds before faith would be possible, and even more evidence would be needed. He would require to thrust a hand into the wound made by the soldier's spear. The idea was stupid. He would never believe! Doubt gave place to anger. Nothing would persuade him that Jesus was alive. He sat alone with his thoughts. The disciples knew it was useless arguing with a stubborn man and unwise to pour oil on a fire! Naaman said he would never wash in the river Jordan, but he did! (2 Kings 5:14). Jonah said he would not preach in Nineveh, but he did! (Jonah 3:4). Simon Peter said he would never deny his Lord, but he did! (Luke 22:55–62). Thomas said: "I will not believe," but he did! (John 20:28).

Thomas the Convinced . . . *How Sublime*

> And after eight days again his disciples were within, and Thomas with them: then came Jesus, the doors being shut, and stood in the midst, and said, Peace be unto you. Then saith he to Thomas, Reach hither thy finger, and behold my hands; and reach hither thy hand, and thrust it into my side: and be not faithless, but believing. And Thomas answered and said unto him, My Lord and my God (John 20:26–28).

Thomas was tired. It had been a long week! The continuing ecstasy of his companions increased his agitation. His world was empty. Yet, he remained among his friends who constantly affirmed Jesus had risen from the dead. As he listened to their testimony and recognized their sincerity, perhaps his resistance began to weaken. But how could the Master be alive, when everyone knew He had died? Then without warning a strange silence filled the room. No one spoke. No one moved. They all heard, "Hello, Thomas." The doubter was amazed and ashamed when he looked at the outstretched hand of the Lord. Tears filled his eyes and joy his soul when he exclaimed, "My Lord and my God." His doubts disappeared. His fingers never touched the nail prints, and his hand never moved to reach the wound in the side of the Savior. He would never repeat his mistake. It is nice to know that Christ is able to meet the challenge of any unbeliever.

Many legends and stories have survived the passing of time, but it would be helpful if the world could be sure of their accuracy. Tradition says that Thomas became a missionary in Parthia, Persia, and India, and there is a place near Madras which is called "Saint Thomas Mount." The discovery of *The Gospel of Thomas* which was found in a jar of papyri at Naj Hamadi, between Cairo and Luxor in 1943, caused international interest. "It took some fourteen years for the knowledge of the discovery to reach the West. Some inkling of *The Gospel of Thomas* had emerged in 1903 from a papyrus discovered by Grenfell and Hunt. The Naj Hamadi document is a collection of 114 sayings of Christ. Some of the quotations differ slightly from those found in the New Testament, and probably represent the views of people who escaped from Jerusalem prior to its fall in 70 A.D. These folk sought refuge in the isolation of a foreign country. Thomas

may indeed have been the author of their original documents."[1]
Thomas would have appreciated the words:

> Doubt sees the obstacles,
> Faith sees the way;
> Doubt sees the darkest night,
> Faith sees the day.
> Doubt dreads to take a step,
> Faith soars on high;
> Doubt questions "Who believes?"
> Faith answers "I."

---

1. *The Pictorial Bible Dictionary* (Nashville: The South Western Company, 1976), 850.

THE DISTINGUISHABLE MARKS OF A CHRISTIAN

By this shall all men know that ye are my disciples
(John 13:35).

I heard the late Dr. John Scroggie tell a thought-provoking story when he was the guest preacher at a youth conference in Aberystwyth, Wales. During his pastorate in London he went to visit a member of his church whom he believed to be a childless widow. She worked for a local match factory making matchboxes by hand. He climbed up many steps to reach the top floor where his friend lived in a small room beneath the roof. She greeted him enthusiastically and after a short conversation said, "Pastor, would you like to see my daughter?" Dr. Scroggie confessed he had no idea she was a mother, but answered, "I would be delighted to meet her." The lady went across to another room and returned, carrying on her outstretched hands the tiny, undeveloped body of her child. The speaker said to his youthful audience, "When I looked into the tiny face, I knew the child had been born an idiot. She had tiny toes, legs, hands and body, but her face was twenty-seven years old. The mother said, 'Pastor, I would not be without her for all the money in the world.'"

The famous preacher appeared to be a little emotional as he remembered the incident, but he continued, "Of course that mother adored her daughter, but would it not have been more wonderful had she been able to look upon a radiant young woman who possessed a very healthy body?" John Scroggie said, "God also has children like that. They were born into His family, but unfortunately never learned to walk and talk; they never developed. The Lord continues to love them with an everlasting love, but would prefer to see them as radiant, energetic Christians." That introduces a very important question. What are the signs by which it is possible to recognize a growing child of the living God? The New Testament supplies at least seven answers.

A Challenging Faith . . . *Accepting Christ*

For God so loved the world, that he gave his only begotten Son, that whosoever believeth in him, should not perish, but have everlasting life (John 3:16).

174

This statement reveals the way souls are born into the family of God. No person is ever naturally born a Christian. All are sinners, and entry into the family of the Lord is only made possible by a spiritual birth. The Gospel is a life-changing message which, when accepted and believed, transforms a sinner into a saint. Old things pass away, and all things become new. Believing the Gospel indicates trust in the Savior, and that initial incident is the first evidence of a new life.

A Close Fellowship . . . *Abiding in Christ*

Abide in me, and I in you. As the branch cannot bear fruit of itself, except it abide in the vine; no more can ye, except ye abide in me (John 15:4).

Christians are said to be *in Christ*; that is, they are joined to Him. A believer does not make a decision and then depart alone to a remote part of God's domain. True disciples are never separated from their Lord—*they abide in Him* as a branch abides in the vine. That union makes possible a flow of divine energy from the Savior to His followers and through them to others. We are unable to produce it; it must emanate from the Lord. There is no substitute for the Holy Spirit. Without His assistance human effort fails. Jesus said, "Without me, ye can do nothing" (John 15:5). *True* Christians can easily be recognized; they are like the Lord.

A Constant Follower . . . *Advancing with Christ*

And he said to them all, If any man will come after me, let him deny himself, and take up his cross daily, and follow me (Luke 9:23).

The evidence of continuing faith is the desire to follow Christ, and the courage to endure hardship. True believers never become tired of the Lord's company. They are consumed by a desire to know more of His Word and sit at His feet. Any person who does not possess an appetite for the bread of life can hardly be a Christian. The cross is the symbol of faith. People who have been to Calvary never refuse to carry their own cross which ultimately will be exchanged for a crown.

A Continuous Faithfulness . . . *Acknowledging Christ*

He that hath my commandments, and keepeth them, he it is
that loveth me (John 14:21).

Unfortunately there are many people who profess to be followers of Christ, but they do not obey His commandments. Probably this is the greatest evidence of Christian growth. It remains
a very important fact that, although God may give life, it is our
responsibility to feed, nourish, and exercise what has been giv-
en. To remain as an undeveloped baby is a tragedy. Our heavenly Father can hardly be proud of anyone who continues to be a
disappointment. John said, "I have no greater joy than to hear
that my children *walk in truth*" (3 John :4). If the apostle could
be disappointed in believers, how much more may God be disturbed by those who fail to live according to their profession.

A Considered Fact . . . *Association with Christ*

I am crucified with Christ: nevertheless I live; yet not I, but
Christ liveth in me: and the life which I now live in the flesh I
live by the faith of the Son of God, who loved me, and gave
himself for me (Gal. 2:20).

Spirit-filled Christians learn how to die! No intelligent, healthy
person wishes to expire. The apostle referred to a different kind
of death, when the self-life is rejected with its inclinations, temp-
tations, and desires. Had the disciples been required to choose
between the excitement and miracles of the Lord's ministry and
His death at Calvary, their choice would have been automatic
and easy. The same fact may be applied to Christians of this age.
To deny the desires of the flesh is difficult. Only consecrated
people welcome identification with Christ in His death.

A Commendable Fervor . . . *Announcing Christ*

But ye shall receive power, after that the Holy Ghost is come
upon you: and ye shall be witnesses unto me both in Jerusalem, and in all Judaea, and in Samaria, and unto the uttermost
part of the earth (Acts 1:8).

When the widow's son at Nain was given a new life, "he that
was dead sat up, *and began to speak*" (Luke 7:15). People who

owe so much to Christ and who seldom, if ever, mention His name, are not consecrated followers. We have a story to tell to the nations, and the glorious privilege of spreading the Gospel is something which all should share. Many believers never have the privilege of traveling overseas to become missionaries, but neighbors are within reach of everybody. When men and women fervently love the Savior, they cannot refrain from mentioning His Name. When folk belong to Christ, they talk about Him, and their testimony is supported by sanctified living.

A Complete Future . . . *Anticipating Christ*

For our conversation [citizenship] is in heaven; from whence also we look for the Savior, the Lord Jesus Christ: Who shall change our vile body, that it may be fashioned like unto his glorious body, according to the working whereby he is able even to subdue all things unto himself (Phil. 3:20–21).

> We are pilgrims pressing onward
> To our home beyond the sky;
> We are each day getting nearer
> To that glorious place on high.
> Earth has lost its gay attraction,
> Heaven alone can satisfy;
> We are going home to glory
> Where we know we'll never die.

Paul was convinced he and his converts could share that certainty. He wrote, "Therefore, my brethren dearly beloved and longed for, my joy and crown, *so stand fast in the Lord*, my dearly beloved" (Phil. 4:1). Likeness to Christ is self-evident; people recognize it before they hear about it!

F. B. Barton, in the year 1914, published a story that he had read in *The Brooklyn Eagle*. It referred to a remarkable incident that had taken place in China. A slave girl was brought to the hospital in Canton. The child was blind and an outcast among her people. She was becoming lame and was of little use to her owner. After an examination, the doctor said she would need an amputation, whereupon the mistress hurriedly left. The girl worked around the hospital but unfortunately contracted leprosy and had to be sent to a leper colony. However, she did not leave as she had

177

arrived. She had heard about the matchless love of Christ, and had become a believer. When she left the hospital, she did not travel alone; the Savior went with her. After two years she had a group of leper Christians around her and in five years had a leper church. Summarizing the complete event, *The Brooklyn Eagle* said: "Today, she is the center of grateful Christian life and service."

That slave girl had no wealth, but she possessed great riches. Many modern Christians have all they need but remain poor. "By this shall all men know that ye are my disciples, *if ye have love one to another*" (John 13:35).

And Saul, yet breathing out threatenings and slaughter against the disciples of the Lord, went unto the high priest, And desired of him letters to Damascus to the synagogues, that if he found any of this way, whether they were men or women, he might bring them bound unto Jerusalem (Acts 9:1–2).

The names given to the early church provide a most interesting Bible study. The followers of Christ were first called disciples (Greek *mattheetes*), because they were pupils or scholars, who, according to the custom of those times, followed their Teacher as He walked and talked along the highways and byways of Palestine. Later, in Antioch, where the disciples had become Christlike, the name was changed to Christians (Acts 11:26). As increasing numbers of converts accepted the new faith, they rejected worldly practices and became members of Christian assemblies. The name "Church" (or *The Ecclesia*), meant "The Called Out Ones." Afterward, the local gatherings of believers were given various names such as *the bride, the building, the body* (Rev. 21:9; Eph. 2:21; 1 Cor. 12:27). From time to time New Testament writers added other names such as "The general assembly and church of the first born, which are written in heaven" (Heb. 12:23). Luke, the beloved physician, was attracted to a special definition. He called the church "*the way*" (Acts 9:1–2). He described how the men in the synagogue at Ephesus spake evil of *that way*, and later, when Demetrius, the silversmith, caused trouble for Paul, it was said: "There was no small stir about *that way*." When Paul addressed the Jewish leaders in Jerusalem he said: "And I persecuted *this way* unto the death" (Acts 22:4). Later he testified before the governor, saying, "But this I confess unto thee, that after *the way* which they call heresy, so worship I the God of my fathers, believing all things which are written in the law and in the prophets" (Acts 24:14). *A way*—a highway always led somewhere, and those who used it knew their destination. Like Abraham, they sought a city! (Heb. 11:8–10).

The Way in Prophecy . . . *Encouraging*

Then the eyes of the blind shall be opened, and the ears of the deaf shall be unstopped. Then shall the lame man leap as an

179

hart, and the tongue of the dumb sing: for in the wilderness shall waters break out, and streams in the desert. . . . And an highway shall be there, and a way, and it shall be called The Way of Holiness; the unclean shall not pass over it; but it shall be for those: the wayfaring men, though fools, shall not err therein. No lion shall be there, nor any ravenous beast shall go up thereon, it shall not be found there; but the redeemed shall walk there: And the ransomed of the Lord shall return, and come to Zion with songs and everlasting joy upon their heads: they shall obtain joy and gladness, and sorrow and sighing shall flee away (Isa. 35:5–10).

During the lifetime of Isaiah the Hebrews resembled the Israel of today. Determined people were endeavoring to establish and strengthen their homeland, while on every side they were confronted by hostile neighbors. The lions and dragons mentioned in the text were synonyms for the kings of adjacent nations. The word picture drawn by Isaiah depicted a land filled with problems where hard-working people, filled with fear and hope, struggled to make a wilderness productive. The thirty-fifth chapter of Isaiah resembles a glorious spring morning after a desolate, unpleasant winter. The prophet looked ahead to the time when the blessings of the Almighty would transform a wilderness into a national paradise. He predicted "the parched ground shall become a pool, and the thirsty land springs of water." The weary people could hardly believe what they heard. "Say to them, that are of a fearful heart, Be strong, fear not: behold, your God shall come with vengeance, even God with a recompense; He will come and save you" (Isa. 35:4).

Today Israel is struggling to survive. Surrounded by hostility, the people face the constant threat of terrorism. Bombs explode, officials are assassinated, and attempts to restore peace appear to be futile. If a modern prophet stood in Jerusalem to repeat the words of Isaiah, he would either be scorned and ridiculed or promoted to the highest level in the legislative assembly of the nation. Yet God's servant was so convinced of the accuracy of his statements that he repeated his prediction. "Therefore the redeemed of the LORD shall return, and come with singing unto Zion; and everlasting joy shall be upon their head: they shall obtain gladness and joy; sorrow and mourning shall flee away" (Isa. 51:11).

It seemed remarkable that in the midst of these promises Isaiah predicted: "And a highway shall be there, and a way, and it shall be called The Way of Holiness." That could hardly be a man-made thoroughfare. It was a way of life, a practice, a system accepted by many people who would embrace holiness. The prophet said this would be evident throughout the restored nation. The way would be used by those people who desired communion with God. That promise has only been partially fulfilled. The future of Israel is bright with prospect and hope. The present outlook may be depressing, but the darkest hour always precedes the dawn.

> Nearer and nearer draws the time,
> The time that shall surely be:
> When the earth shall be filled
> With the glory of God,
> As the waters cover the sea.

The Way in Person ... *Enthralling*

Thomas saith unto him, Lord, we know not whither thou goest; and how can we know the way? Jesus saith unto him, I am the way, the truth, and the life: No man cometh unto the Father but by me (John 14:5–6).

The disciples were confused. They anticipated a kingdom in which Jesus would be the King of Kings. But apparently the Savior had other ideas. He spoke of building many mansions and indicated He was about to accept an assignment in which He would be a Master-Builder. He said,

"Let not your heart be troubled: ye believe in God, believe also in me. In my Father's house are many mansions: if it were not so, I would have told you. I go to prepare a place for you. And if I go and prepare a place for you, I will come again and receive you unto myself; that where I am, there ye may be also. And whither I go ye know, and the way ye know. Thomas saith unto him, Lord, we know not whither thou goest; and how can we know the way?" (John 14:1–5).

The idea of owning a home in God's country was attractive, but how to reach and inhabit that property presented problems.

181

"Master, how may we reach that heavenly location?" Jesus replied, "Through Me; I am the way." When the Lord made that statement, He probably remembered the words spoken by Isaiah: "And an highway shall be there and a way, and it shall be called The Way of Holiness; the unclean shall not pass over it, but it shall be for those: the wayfaring men, though fools, shall not err therein." The Savior was the fulfillment of that prediction. He was the highway along which sinners would reach their eternal abode. Isaiah 35:8–10 is filled with promises concerning the Messiah. There are nine informative milestones along the royal highway.

The Special Way

"And an highway shall be there and a way." That these terms should be coupled together is most suggestive. *A way* in olden days was used by everyone. *A highway* was a special road made for and used by a king. Such roads were made at the ruler's command and reserved for the royal chariots. Isaiah predicted God would create a special highway that would be open for all travelers.

The Saintly Way

"And it shall be called the way of holiness." The statement "the unclean could not pass over it," suggests that nothing that defiled would be permitted to contaminate the highway. The royal Builder of the thoroughfare would welcome sinners and do for them what others could not do. His precious blood would remove their sins.

The Separated Way

"The unclean shall not pass over it." The highway automatically separated people into two communities. Those who complied with and others who ignored the regulations. The unclean who sought cleansing would be permitted to travel on the road to glory. Others who preferred to remain unclean would travel another road, in another direction, to disaster. During the ministry of the Lord Jesus the separating influence of His message became increasingly apparent. He said those who were not for Him were against Him.

182

The Simple Way

"It shall be for those the wayfaring men." Even peasants, farm laborers, and other ordinary folk would be permitted to use the highway. Academic degrees, social greatness, eminence of any kind would not be necessary for travelers. Children, hoboes, all who so desired could enter, for in assessing greatness, God was more concerned with purity of heart than social distinction.

The Sure Way

"Fools shall not err therein." These travelers, unable to distinguish themselves in other walks of life, could cover themselves with glory on the road to heaven. God does not always choose the great, the mighty. Sometimes He chooses the foolish things of this world to confound the wise.

The Safe Way

"No lion shall be there, nor any ravenous beast shall go up thereon." The lion in ancient times was considered to be the most ravenous and ferocious of all animals. Its presence in any vicinity threatened travelers with death. The royal highway would be protected by soldiers. Every enemy would be chased away to guarantee the protection of the king's friends.

The Salvation Way

"The redeemed shall walk there." Redemption was an experience known by people who had been sold into slavery and later redeemed. The Prince of glory came to earth to save sinners, to emancipate those who had been in bondage. Paul said, "In whom we have redemption through his blood, the forgiveness of sins, according to the riches of his grace" (Eph. 1:7).

The Singing Way

"And the ransomed of the Lord shall return and come to Zion with songs and everlasting joy upon their heads." Happy people sing. The forgiveness of sins is the forerunner of increasing happiness. The breaking of the chains of bondage is a cause for praise. The opening of the doors of a prison is a prelude to a shout of victory. Heaven will be filled with choirs singing the song of Moses and the Lamb (Rev. 5:9).

183

"They shall obtain joy and gladness and sorrow and sighing shall flee away." Thus will eternity begin for travelers reaching their destination. Isaiah looked ahead to the highway which God would make possible; we look back to Jesus, the fulfillment of every prediction, the joy of His people, the consummation of our greatest hopes.[1]

The Way in Practice . . . *Enriching*

It should not be a cause for amazement that the members of the early church were called "followers of the Way." They believed the Savior was the divinely appointed path by which men and women obtained access to God. They loved the Lord, who had volunteered to be their Companion and Guide as they continued their journey toward heaven. It was a very appropriate definition, for the Lord had said, "No man cometh unto the Father, but by me" (John 14:6). The writer to the Hebrews said, "Having therefore, brethren, boldness to enter into the holiest by the blood of Jesus. By a new and living way, which he hath consecrated for us, through the veil, that is to say, his flesh; And having an high priest over the house of God; Let us draw near with a true heart" (Heb. 10:19–22).

When Paul sought authorization for his mission to Damascus, it was not easy to define the limits of his search. The name "Christian" had not been given to any people. The church was in its infancy. He could only ask about folk who subscribed to *The Way*. Any person who knew about the whereabouts of such men or women must have some knowledge of the Nazarene. Throughout Paul's stay in Ephesus, the enemies of the faith constantly denounced *The Way* (Acts 19:9, 23). His teaching offended both Jews and Gentiles. The Hebrews recognized only Jehovah, but the Gentiles worshiped many gods. The new doctrines contradicted the faith of everybody outside of the Christian church. Jesus said access to the Almighty was only possible through Him, and therefore the Jews believed the Lord to be a blasphemer worthy of death. They said to Pilate, "We have a law, and by our law he ought to die, because he made himself the Son of God" (John 19:7).

Everything Jesus did and said appeared to contradict the traditions of the elders. In more senses than one, old things were

184

passing away, and everything was becoming new. He opened the way for all men to pray and not to be dependent upon a high priest who could only approach God once every year. Christ opened a highway which welcomed Samaritans and Gentiles of all races. The Hebrews believed all non-Jews were outcasts, dogs, undesirable. The Lord also created a way by which even women were recognized for their true worth. They were daughters of Jehovah, not objects of passion to be exploited by men. Jesus also opened the minds of people, for He taught that all men, however significant their academic excellence, needed to be as little children in order to enter the kingdom of God. He taught that humility was better than pride, virtue superseded vice, and to be a doorkeeper in the house of the Lord was more to be desired than riches. To belong to *The Way* indicated a traveler subscribed to those ideas. Today people speak of Baptists, Methodists, Anglicans, Presbyterians, and Catholics, yet long ago there was only *one church*—it was called *The Way*. Its members believed and obeyed the commandments of their Master. Unfortunately, with the passing of time theologians argued about doctrine, and branch roads were made from the main highway. These led to confusion, heresy, and failure. Someday there will be but one road again. Perhaps it will be called *The Way*—it will lead to the Lamb.

---

1.   Ivor Powell, *John's Wonderful Gospel* (Grand Rapids: Kregel Publications, 1987), 297–300.

Philippi, which is the chief city of that part of Macedonia, and a colony: and we were in that city abiding certain days. And on the sabbath we went out of the city by a river side, where prayer was wont to be made; and we sat down, and spake unto the women which resorted thither. And a certain woman named Lydia, a seller of purple, of the city of Thyatira, which worshipped God, heard us; whose heart the Lord opened, that she attended unto the things which were spoken by Paul (Acts 16:12–15).

Among modern churches meetings specially convened for ladies are commonplace. Yet it is surprising to learn that throughout the Bible only one gathering of this type is mentioned. It was a service probably held every sabbath on the banks of the river at Philippi. It was one of the most important meetings connected with the early church. Its influence reached the entire world.

When Paul and Silas reached Philippi, they sought a place to stay and then began to make inquiries about the city—it was their first visit. Paul usually began his ministry in the local synagogue, but there was no such place in Philippi. If ten Jews lived in a community, they could legally establish a place of worship. The fact that there were fewer than the required number suggests Philippi was a Gentile city. Perhaps that explains why Caesar had built a garrison in the vicinity. The soldiers were there to protect Roman inhabitants. Paul must have been disappointed to learn of the scarcity of Jews, but someone informed him that every sabbath women held a prayer meeting on the banks of the river. Paul and his companions decided to attend to find out what was happening. The ladies who were present that day were astonished to see men approaching along the river bank and sitting down in their midst. Evidently the newcomers intended to stay for the whole meeting. Strangers in such a situation were always invited to participate, and when asked, Paul began to address the audience. Soon the face of a woman named Lydia began to glow, and later she requested to be baptized. Perhaps God smiled, for this was the climax of a very long process arranged in heaven. It might be easier to understand and appreciate this lady if we seek answers to certain questions.

Who Was Lydia, and What Had Happened to Her?

Luke says she was a native of Thyatira, an important center for the dyeing of cloth and the manufacture of fine garments. Within the city were the headquarters of a very famous Guild of Dyers, and Lydia might have had connections with that organization. Apparently her husband had died. She was a widow, a Gentile by birth. Although she may have formally worshiped idols, she had become a convert to the Jewish faith. She was a proselyte. Evidently she had passed through a great crisis that left her devastated. If that time of testing were associated with the death of her husband, it would be easy to understand her predicament. She became a worried soul in search of peace.

Why Did She Leave Her Home in Thyatira?

Certain reasons might have accounted for her decision. (1) If she had renounced her idolatry to be identified with Jehovah, many of her former associates might accuse her of being a religious traitor. (2) The members of the Guild of Dyers might use their influence to persuade customers to purchase goods from others who were faithful to the gods. That could lead to bankruptcy. On the other hand, that same organization might have appointed this gifted woman to be their representative in an effort to extend trade relations. Perhaps the most convincing reason for her departure was the overruling grace of God. Lydia was destined to have a far-reaching ministry which would have been impossible had she remained in her native city.

Why Did She Decide to Go to Philippi—600 Miles Away?

Philippi was the chief city in Macedonia. It was inhabited mostly by Gentiles, and many soldiers were stationed in the local Roman garrison. Military men were always looking for unusual gifts to take to their families and friends. The prospects for increasing business were excellent, and through the coming and going of military men there existed the chance of reaching the entire Roman Empire. Furthermore, since Philippi was far removed from Thyatira, Lydia would be a stranger, and repercussions from enemies were unlikely to occur. She could live without fear of recrimination. There is reason to believe that, above all else, God was fulfilling His own purpose.

Why Did Lydia Begin Attending a Ladies' Prayer Meeting?

This woman was not only a convert to Judaism, she was also a very sincere soul searching for peace. When she arrived in the city, she purchased a large house, and this suggests she was either a wealthy woman or was sponsored by the Guild which had sent her to increase their business. When the lady discovered there was no synagogue, she wondered how she could possibly exist without a sanctuary. It is not known whether or not she commenced the sabbath service, but in any case, Lydia became one of the women who regularly attended. At the weekly meeting the women sang some of the songs of Israel and then discussed important parts of the sacred writings. Lydia still hungered for something of which she had no knowledge. Only people who have known that yearning can appreciate the struggle within her soul.

Why Did She Ask to Be Baptized?

When she watched with speculative eyes the visiting men sitting among the congregation, she wondered what they desired and what they would say. It is not difficult to understand what was said by Paul, for whenever he preached to people for the first time, he followed the same pattern. It is safe to assume all the women were Jewish, and, recognizing that fact, Paul would describe his own experiences. His testimony of being employed by the high priest in Jerusalem would at least be interesting. The story of his encounter with the risen Christ would introduce his new faith that Jesus was the Messiah. When he explained how the deepest yearning of his hungry soul had been satisfied in Christ, Lydia suddenly realized he was speaking to her. When her soul responded, it became evident the Spirit of God was leading her to the kingdom of God. Salvation is not the exercise of a religious ordinance, but an encounter with the risen Lord. She already knew the significance of baptism for she had become a proselyte, and no Gentile was ever accepted into Judaism until they had been immersed as a confession that he or she was abandoning idols to worship Jehovah. Lydia announced to everyone that she was forsaking everything to become a Christian.

What Happened in Her Home?

Probably she was immersed immediately in the nearby river,

and afterward she said to Paul, "If ye have judged me faithful to the Lord, come into my house and abide there." "She earnestly entreated us," Luke said. "The Lord opened her heart," but she opened her home. Gratitude always gives! After Paul and Silas were released from prison, they were instructed by the magistrates to leave the city immediately, but Paul refused to do this. It was significant that he went first to the home of Lydia to comfort and strengthen *the brethren*. Men were already associating with the new movement. Possibly, the jailer and his family were among the first to do this.

It is thought-provoking that Luke came to Philippi with Paul and Silas, but he did not leave with them. Later when he wrote the Acts of the Apostles, he said: "And *they* went out of the prison, and entered into the house of Lydia: and when *they* had seen the brethren, *they* comforted them, and departed" (Acts 16:40). Paul recognized the need of someone to help the young converts, and it seems Luke stayed behind to become the pastor of the first church in Philippi. There was no other suitable place where those early Christians could assemble. It was providential that Lydia had bought a large house.

Why Did Lydia Continue to Give So Much?

When Paul left Philippi, he ultimately arrived in Thessalonica. The journey could not have taken longer than a few days. Yet even in that short space of time the apostle received two love-gifts from the church in Philippi. Long afterward he remembered the assistance received from those people and wrote, "Now ye Philippians know also, that in the beginning of the gospel . . . no church communicated with me as concerning giving and receiving, but ye only. For even in Thessalonica ye sent *once and again* unto my necessity" (Phil. 4:15–16). This generosity continued throughout the life and ministry of the apostle. Probably Lydia spoke to her brothers and sisters in Christ and suggested it would be nice to send help to their beloved Paul. This was a great way to express their appreciation. Consecrated souls are never stingy! Longfellow was one of Britain's greatest poets. His work never deteriorated. Toward the end of his life he was asked what was the secret of his continuing success. Pointing to an apple tree, he replied, "That apple tree is very old, but I never saw greater blossoms than those it carried this year. That tree grows a little new wood each year, and the wood produces the flowers. I try to grow some new wood each year, and this explains my success." Probably Lydia did the same kind of thing. Her love gifts to Paul expressed the gratitude in her soul. She influenced the entire world with her dedicated service.

What Kind of Welcome Did She Receive in Heaven?

If Paul's homegoing to heaven preceded Lydia's it would be easy to imagine his taking her by the hand to say, "Master, she is home at last. I could not have accomplished my mission without her help." And the Lord would respond, saying, "Well done, thou good and faithful servant. Enter thou into the joy of thy Lord." It would be nice to know what kind of reception we shall have when we stand before God's throne.

But when Peter was come to Antioch, I withstood him to the face, because he was to be blamed. For before that certain came from James, he did eat with the Gentiles: but when they were come, he withdrew and separated himself, fearing them which were of the circumcision. And the other Jews dissembled likewise with him; insomuch that Barnabas also was carried away with their dissimulation (Gal. 2:11–13).

When a hammer strikes an anvil, sparks are to be expected. This was true when the very indignant Paul condemned the illustrious Simon Peter before the elders in the church at Antioch. The Lord gave to Simon the name Cephas, which meant "The Rock," but unfortunately a tide of circumstance had undermined that rock, and it was being dislodged. When Paul heard of Peter's actions he was very annoyed, and could hardly wait to meet the offending brother. When Simon arrived in Antioch, Paul was ready to challenge his disgraceful conduct, and repercussions of the confrontation disturbed all the assemblies.

Simon Peter was just a piece of human clay transformed by the Master Potter. He was ordinary like his admirers. He could soar to the top of life's mountain, but he could also be affected by fogs of disappointment and fear. Probably he meant well, but sometimes he was unreliable and infuriating. He was too concerned with the attitude of other people, and this led to disaster. Simon had been impulsive when he left the fishing boat and walked on the water to go to Jesus and desperate when he began to sink. Peter was nervous and apprehensive when challenged by a maid at the trial of the Savior, yet overconfident when the Lord predicted approaching danger. He was God's wonderful spokesman at Pentecost, but later his compromising behavior aroused Paul's indignation and caused dismay among Gentile Christians. Peter was a man of moods. As was said of Elijah, he "was a man subject to like passions as we are" (see James 5:17). Nevertheless, God used him mightily, and that supplies hope for everybody.

An Unfortunate Compromise . . . *Dangerous*

There is reason to believe Simon Peter was the most popular

man among the original disciples, and that appealed to Gentile Christians. Each time he testified concerning his visit to Cornelius, a Gentile, they were delighted. Peter knew they were not unclean. When he visited their homes to share a meal, they felt honored in entertaining such an illustrious brother. Even Paul was pleased that bigotry had been expelled from the soul of his colleague. Then came the day when things began to change. Legalists from Jerusalem were about to visit the church, and their unyielding attitude regarding Mosaic law was recognized everywhere. Peter frowned. The visitors belonged to the head church, and their influence could cause problems. Simon began to cancel his appointments with Gentiles. He made all kinds of excuses, and his new friends became suspicious. When he "withdrew" himself and ignored them when they passed in the street, it became evident he had changed. When Paul heard of Peter's behavior, resentment filled his soul. Once again the offender was concerned about the opinions of people and had lost sight of his Lord. Uncertainty began to intimidate the church. The unity of believers was being threatened. A friend had forsaken them. Their champion had become an advocate of circumcision, and they feared that Gentiles would soon be considered second-class citizens within the assembly. Paul was annoyed! His eyes were steel, his heart aflame with indignation. He was determined to give Peter a piece of his mind!

An Unprecedented Confrontation . . . *Determined*

> But when Peter was come to Antioch, I withstood him to the face, because he was to be blamed (Gal. 2:11).

The Lord had given advice concerning methods by which problems between two church members should be solved:

> Moreover if thy brother shall trespass against thee, go and tell him his fault between thee and him alone: if he shall hear thee, thou hast gained thy brother. But if he will not hear thee, then take with thee one or two more, that in the mouth of two or three witnesses every word may be established. And if he shall neglect to hear them, tell it unto the church: but if he neglect to hear the church, let him be unto thee as an heathen man and a publican (Matt. 18:15–17).

192

Evidently Paul was impatient. He was in a hurry! He believed that a straight line was the shortest distance between two points, and the best way to solve a problem was to go straight to the heart of the matter. This incident was not a slight headache affecting the comfort of the assembly; it was a swiftly moving cancer that could destroy the church. Simon Peter needed surgery. The situation demanded immediate action. There was no time to appoint committees that would argue forever. This promised to be a battle, and Paul was ready to defend his convictions not only against Simon Peter, but against the devil himself. Years later he wrote: "But when I saw that they walked not uprightly according to the truth of the gospel, I said unto Peter *before them all . . .* " (Gal. 2:14).

Probably the meeting place was packed to capacity with apprehensive listeners. They expected verbal fireworks and were not disappointed.

An Unmerciful Condemnation . . . *Deadly*

If thou [Peter], being a Jew, livest after the manner of the Gentiles, and not as do the Jews, why compellest thou the Gentiles to live as do the Jews? We who are Jews by nature . . . Knowing that a man is not justified by the works of the law, but by the faith of Jesus Christ, even we have believed in Jesus Christ, that we might be justified by the faith of Christ, and not by the works of the law: for by the works of the law shall no flesh be justified" (Gal. 2:14–16).

My brother you are trying to restore that which the Savior destroyed. Your words may be eloquent, but they are spoken by hypocritical lips. You told us that the Master instructed you to proceed to the home of Cornelius because those Gentiles had been cleansed by God, even though they had never been circumcised. You were instructed not to call unclean those whom God had cleansed (see Acts 10:15). Consequently, you proceeded with your mission and have since enjoyed fellowship with many other Gentiles. Then the legalists from Jerusalem scared you half to death! Why did you treat your brethren as strangers? Did you have cataracts on your eyes when you pretended not to see them in the streets? Simon Peter, you preach one thing but practice another. What kind of leadership are you supplying to the church?

You are supposed to be The Rock but are more like shifting sand, blown about by every wind of doctrine. If we are to judge by your recent conduct, then you have forfeited the right to be a shepherd of God's flock. Are you now telling us that the death of Christ is insufficient to guarantee our acceptance with God? Are you suggesting that unless men subscribe to the rite of circumcision, not even the precious blood of Christ can remove their sins? Did observance to the Mosaic law bring peace to your soul? You are an unreliable leader, and the whole church knows that is true. It was not the law that saved you, but acceptance of Jesus as your Lord and Master. My brother, He not only lifted you from the waters of the Sea of Galilee, He rescued you from many other weaknesses which threatened to overwhelm your soul. Simon Peter, it is difficult to avoid the conclusion that you are a very poor example of the faith once for all delivered to the saints.

An Unforeseen Climax . . . *Delightful*

Be diligent that ye may be found of him in peace, without spot, and blameless. And account that the long suffering of our Lord is salvation; even as our beloved brother Paul also according to the wisdom given unto him hath written unto you; As also in all his epistles, speaking in them of these things (2 Peter 3:14–16).

Simon Peter possessed a volcanic soul that could erupt at any moment. It would be interesting to know his reactions to the charges made against him. He had been humiliated before the entire church and could have condemned his accuser for not following the procedure suggested by the Lord. Even if Paul were correct, these deliberations could have been held secretly, so that unbelievers would not criticize the church.

It may be significant that no mention is made of Peter's retaliation. If the Scriptures are to be our guide, then it must be assumed he did not reply. Did he acknowledge his mistake and ask for forgiveness? It is unwise to speculate about matters concerning which no information is available. Many people would have been resentful and would have carried a grudge. Peter was not that type of man. Later, when he wrote to his friends, he referred to his former antagonist as *our beloved brother Paul.*

He also acknowledged the wisdom which God had given in the writing of Paul's epistles. He appreciated everything his colleague had accomplished in preaching the Gospel and was proud to be associated with the man who had accomplished so much for the Lord.

The introductory salutation of his second letter revealed that he and Paul believed the same Gospel.

Simon Peter, a servant and an apostle of Jesus Christ, to them that have obtained like precious faith with us through the righteousness of God and our Saviour Jesus Christ (2 Peter 1:1).

The apostle was now a mature saint who wrote about precious facts.

The Precious Trial of Faith (1 Peter 1:7)
The Precious Blood (1 Peter 1:19)
The Precious Corner Stone (1 Peter 2:6)
The Precious Savior (1 Peter 2:7)
The Precious Promises (2 Peter 1:4)

It is never easy for a strong man to admit failure. It is to be expected that he will try to justify his conduct. That Peter refused to permit prejudice to destroy his admiration of Paul must be one of his most delightful accomplishments. Peter deserves the place he occupies in the affections of all Christians.

The love of Christ, which passeth knowledge
(Eph. 3:19).

Since the beginning of the Christian era preachers have tried to express the wonder of the love of Christ, yet all would agree this cannot be expressed in words. When Paul wrote to the Ephesian Christians, he hoped they would "be able to comprehend with all saints what is the *breadth*, and *length*, and *depth*, and *height*; And to know the love of Christ which passeth knowledge" (Eph. 3:18–19). Even the apostle admitted what he desired would be impossible. How can any man know something which is beyond knowledge? He spoke of the breadth, length, depth, and height, but one might ask, how are those dimensions measured? The scientists speak of eternity in terms of space as well as time. If their conclusions be correct, even height baffles comprehension. The poet wrote:

> Could we with ink the ocean fill,
> And were the skies of parchment made,
> Were every stalk on earth a quill,
> And every man a scribe by trade,
> To write the love of God above,
> Would drain the ocean dry.
> Nor could the scroll contain the whole,
> Though stretched from sky to sky.

The Bible described the love of God, the Savior manifested it, and men talk about it. Divine love as seen in Christ was and is still the greatest power in the world. Seven incidents in the New Testament describe the great compassion of the Lord.

Compassion Caring

But when he [Christ] saw the multitudes, he was moved with compassion on them, because they fainted, and were scattered abroad, as sheep having no shepherd (Matt. 9:36).

Increasing excitement had gripped the citizens of Palestine. The appearance of a strange preacher had stirred their emotions. They had temporarily abandoned their daily routine and left everything to follow Jesus. He was different from any other speaker. He uttered words of profound wisdom, and healed sick people. From all parts of the country crowds had come, and the future promised to be thrilling. Fishing boats were high and dry on the beaches, and even their owners seemed unconcerned that their livelihood was in jeopardy. Life was at a standstill. People needed to return to their homes, but were reluctant to leave— they might miss something! The women with children were becoming anxious, and food was in short supply. The desire to remain with the Savior was irresistible.

"But when he saw the multitudes, he was moved with compassion on them, because they fainted, and were scattered abroad as sheep having no shepherd." The Lord understood the predicament; they were tired, and the children were restless. Jesus appreciated the difficulty, and His love overflowed—"He was moved with compassion."

Robert Harkness evidently considered this great fact when he wrote:

> Does Jesus care when my heart is pained
> Too deeply for mirth or song?
> As the burdens press, and cares distress,
> And the way seems weary and long?
> Oh yes, He cares; I know He cares;
> His heart is touched with my grief:
> When the days are weary, the long nights dreary,
> I know my Saviour cares.

Compassion Curing

And Jesus went forth, and saw a great multitude, and was moved with compassion toward them, and he healed their sick (Matt. 14:14).

Matthew explained that Jesus was filled with compassion because the people were as sheep without a shepherd. They had no leader to provide sustenance for their souls. This fact was accentuated when John the Baptist was murdered. He had been a faithful witness, and his great meetings in the Jordan Valley were destined to be remembered forever. His death meant that only Jesus remained to supply the Bread of Life. The wilderness preacher had accurately predicted his demise when he said, "He [Christ] must increase, I must decrease." When John's disciples described their master's funeral, the Savior felt the need of being alone with God. He stepped into a small boat and prepared to sail to an uninhabited place somewhere along the shore of the Sea of Galilee where He could be free from clamoring crowds. His plans were never fulfilled, for when the boat approached the shoreline, people who had walked around the head of the lake were waiting to greet Him. Their faith and hope were clearly expressed when they placed sick friends at His feet. They had arrived at the same conclusion which made Simon Peter say, "Lord, to whom shall we go? thou hast the words of eternal life" (John 6:68). Jesus knew the people were dependent upon His kindness. He could not disappoint them. "He healed their sick." The sun was beginning to set when "the Sun of Righteousness arose with healing in his wings" (see Mal. 4:2).

Perhaps it was significant that Jesus healed the sick before He fed the multitude. Some of the participants might not have enjoyed their food had they been worrying whether or not their journey had been in vain. Ultimately, the meal became a joyful thanksgiving banquet, and perhaps the happiest one sharing the provision was the Lord Himself.

Compassion Considering

> Then Jesus called his disciples unto him, and said, I have compassion on the multitude, because they continue with me now three days, and have nothing to eat: and I will not send them away fasting, lest they faint in the way (Matt. 15:32).

The crowd was overwhelmingly enthusiastic. The people had followed Jesus for three days. They were hungry, but no one complained. Their patience had been rewarded when the Savior healed all types of diseases. Matthew said "great multitudes came unto him, having with them those that were lame, blind, dumb, maimed, and many others, and cast them down at Jesus' feet; and he healed them." Language could not express the extent of the people's enthusiasm. They had witnessed sights at which angels would rejoice. Even the need for food was temporarily forgotten as they watched the miracles of Jesus.

Nevertheless, the Lord was greatly concerned. When other

men might have rejoiced at the unprecedented acclamation, He thought of the fatigue that threatened His congregation. Children were hungry, mothers were becoming anxious, and even men ran the risk of collapsing as they journeyed homeward. Even spiritual ecstasy cannot prevent physical exhaustion. The people needed nourishment.

Jesus was a very considerate leader. When the disciples might have been irritable because of continuous pressure, the Lord remained calm and dignified. He thought only of other people. To prevent a forthcoming problem, He prepared a banquet in the wilderness. Believing that prevention is better than cure, He fed the congregation and provided the strength necessary for their immediate future. Jesus met their past needs when he healed the sick, their present needs when He fed the hungry, and the future necessity by supplying strength to go home.

Sometimes God's children worry unnecessarily. They become anxious about things that never happen. The miracle of the loaves and fishes demonstrated His ability to understand future problems and assist His trusting followers.

Compassion Cooperating

And behold, two blind men sitting by the way side, when they heard that Jesus passed by, cried out, saying, Have mercy on us, O Lord, thou Son of David. And the multitude rebuked them, because they should hold their peace: but they cried the more, saying, Have mercy on us, O Lord, thou Son of David. And Jesus stood still, and called them, and said, What will ye that I shall do unto you? They say unto him, Lord, that our eyes might be opened. So Jesus had compassion on them, and touched their eyes: and immediately their eyes received sight, and they followed him (Matt. 20:30–34).

They were beggars, two blind men who hoped people would be generous. Deprived of their vision, they had become accustomed to living in darkness. The psalmist said, "The heavens declare the glory of God; and the firmament sheweth his handiwork" (Ps. 19:1), but unfortunately the beggars could not read the message in the sky. If they had been born blind, they had never seen the stars. If they had become blind, they could only rely on memories of the past. Some sightless men could have been prosperous, but others sat hopelessly in darkness. Even money could not compensate for their affliction.

Today something special was taking place. Many people were in the street, and the beggars expectantly held out their hands. Probably the crowds were not interested; their attention was elsewhere. When the men were informed that Jesus, the Healer from Nazareth, was passing by, they began to shout, "Have mercy on us, thou Son of David." Their piercing cries were heard above the clamor of the people who immediately complained, telling them to be quiet. They probably said, "Hold your peace. That rabbi cannot be bothered by beggars." "But they cried the more. . . . And Jesus stood still, and called them, and said, What will ye that I shall do unto you?" Had those desperate men been influenced by the crowd or permitted doubt to silence their request, they would have remained in the dark. That Jesus heard and responded to the cry for help, provided convincing evidence that God who sees a wounded sparrow falling to the ground (see Matt. 10:29) could also hear cries for help even above the clamor of excited people.

> Prayer is the soul's sincere desire,
> Uttered or unexpressed:
> The motion of a hidden fire,
> That trembles in the breast.
>
> Prayer is the simplest form of speech,
> That infant lips can try;
> Prayer the sublimest strains that reach
> The Majesty on high.
>
> O Thou, by whom we come to God;
> The life, the truth, the way:
> The path of prayer Thyself hast trod:
> Lord, teach us how to pray.
> James Montgomery, 1771–1854

Compassion Cleansing

And Jesus, moved with compassion, put forth his hand, and touched him, and saith unto him, I will; be thou clean (Mark 1:41).

Lepers were the most pitiable beggars in Palestine. Their disease separated them from family and friends, robbed them of employment, and made them forfeit everything of value. Banished to a life of despair and loneliness, they were dependent on relatives to bring food and could only hope a premature death would terminate their sufferings. It was never revealed where this leper lived nor how he heard of the approach of Jesus, but evidently he had been stirred by the possibility of cleansing. He left wherever he was and, drawing near to the Lord, begged for assistance. His faith in the ability of Christ never wavered, but he was not sure Jesus would be willing to grant the favor. He said, "*If thou wilt*—thou canst make me clean." Defying the teachings and beliefs of the nation, the Lord touched the suppliant, which was forbidden by law.

Jesus was filled with compassion when He saw a person who was waiting to die, a derelict without a friend, a pauper without money. He knew what man was meant to be, and when He saw the extent of the tragedy before Him, he was "moved with compassion." This was not necessary. His word would have been sufficient to banish the disease. Even the leper could hardly believe his eyes. He could not remember when he had last been touched by anyone. Jesus was not only a great healer, He was a fearless friend. At first the man could hardly believe what had happened, but when Christ commanded him to go to the priest, it was evident a miracle had been performed. In spite of the command to be silent, the fellow was so exuberant he began to tell everybody about the transformation in his life. It is difficult to condemn his actions, for had we been in a similar position, we also might have acted unwisely. The cleansed leper would have appreciated the hymn:

> He touched me, O, He touched me,
> And O, the joy that floods my soul;
> Something happened, and now I know,
> He touched me and made me whole.

Compassion Conquering

Jesus . . . saith unto him, Go home to thy friends, and tell them how great things the Lord hath done for thee, and hath had compassion on thee (Mark 5:19).

201

The account of the Savior's visit to Gadara is strangely interesting, for He knew the people would be antagonistic. Scared they might suffer additional financial losses, the men asked Him to leave the area before further damage was done. The disciples might have considered the journey to have been a waste of precious time, but the Lord accomplished what He came to do. He delivered a soul from the bondage of Satan, and that man was soon to become the bearer of good tidings to an entire community. There is reason to believe that Jesus deliberately made the journey to meet the demoniac who lived among the tombs. Elsewhere the Lord ministered to multitudes of people. In the cemetery at Gadara, he spoke to one, or two demoniacs (see Matt. 8:28), but that fact teaches how He evaluated the worth of a man. The Savior believed the reclamation of one soul was more to be desired than any material gain possible to human beings.

It is interesting that Jesus made that journey to meet the need of a demoniac. Would it not have been more rewarding to deliver hundreds of sick folk at great meetings in Capernaum? It is the desire of God that all men should hear the good news of salvation. If people cannot come to Him, He will go to them. He loved those unfortunate men, and His amazing power liberated them from the bondage of evil. Had He opposed the attitude of His critics, an altercation might have arisen which would have left scars upon the conscience of the community. Wisely, Jesus instructed His convert to return to the village and testify concerning the compassion shown to him. He knew the man would be faithful to his commission. It is stimulating to remember the power of the Savior was equal to any and every challenge. Many years have passed since that memorable moment on the hillside of Gadara, but the ability of the Lord has never diminished.

Compassion Comforting

And it came to pass the day after, that he went into a city called Nain; and many of his disciples went with him, and much people. Now when he came nigh to the gate of the city, behold, there was a dead man carried out, the only son of his mother, and she was a widow: and much people of the city was with her. And when the Lord saw her, he had compassion on her, and said unto her, Weep not (Luke 7:11–13).

202

This poor woman probably wished she were dead! Her husband had died leaving her to care for her child, and now her son had died. Why had God permitted this to happen? Why had He not completed His work by taking her? She was beyond words and tears. The time for the hastily arranged funeral had arrived. She was expected to follow her boy to his last resting place. The sad event had aroused the sympathy of the entire city, and while funerals were generally attended by only family and neighbors, this one was different—"Much people of the city was with her." Sadly, with bowed head and aching heart, she followed the bier down the narrow street.

Then suddenly the procession came to a halt. Something had stopped the progress of the mourners. A Stranger had interfered. The men carrying the body were motionless. Who was this Man, and by what authority had He halted the funeral march? The distressed mother looked up and saw the Stranger gazing intently at her, and then a mystical warmth began to remove the chill from her soul.

> And when the Lord saw her, he had compassion on her, and said unto her, Weep not. And he came and touched the bier, and they that bare him [the corpse] stood still. And he said, Young man, I say unto thee, Arise. And he that was dead, sat up, and began to speak. And he [Jesus] delivered him to his mother. And there came a fear on all: and they glorified God, saying, That a great prophet is risen up among us; that God hath visited his people (Luke 7:13–16).

Perhaps the Savior thought of His own mother when he saw the woman who had twice been bereaved. This was His only recorded visit to Nain, and He arrived at the exact moment when the funeral was passing through the gate. Had Jesus been a few minutes earlier or later, He could have missed that funeral. His timing was perfect—it always is!

GRADUATING FROM GOD'S ACADEMY OF GRACE

Let us go on unto perfection (Heb. 6:1).

Space rockets are designed to explore the sky. Tremendous amounts of money and time are given to the project, for man hopes outer space will come within reach of earth. Similarly, Christians are meant to reach unlimited heights of spirituality and behold the wonders of God's sufficiency. When for one reason or another rockets fail to justify their existence, scientists suffer intense disappointment.

There are three kinds of space vehicles which suggest counterparts within the church. First, there is the rocket that fails to leave the ground. It never realizes its potential. It never flies. Secondly, there is the rocket that survives its countdown and ignition, flies for a time, then falls into oblivion. Thirdly, there is the vehicle that continues to ascend, and the higher it goes the more detailed are the pictures transmitted back to earth. Within every church, these types are found. Certain people profess faith but do not continue. Others exhibit great enthusiasm but after a short time their continuance abruptly terminates. There are some who continue to function, and the success of their efforts provides the utmost satisfaction. To change the simile, it might be said that within God's academy certain achievements precede graduation, and these are clearly defined in the Scriptures.

Looking at Christ . . . *Confidently Welcoming*

The next day John seeth Jesus coming unto him, and saith, Behold, the Lamb of God, which taketh away the sin of the world (John 1:29).

John the Baptist was a special man chosen by God to be the herald of the King of Kings. His birth and early training were ordained by Jehovah, and in many senses he resembled Samuel who grew up under the supervision of the high priest. It was never revealed what happened in the desert, nor how God communicated with His young servant, but later in his life John confessed: "And I knew him not: but he that sent me to baptize with water, the same said unto me, Upon whom thou shalt see the Spirit descending, and remaining on him, *the same is he* which baptizeth with the Holy Ghost. And I saw, and bare record that this is the Son of God" (John 1:33–34).

The wilderness preacher had keen eyesight, and every day his eyes scanned the crowds. He was not aware of the identity of the Messiah, but anticipated His arrival. Then, one day he saw the Man from Nazareth, and it was as though a light had been turned on in his brain. When he saw the dove descending to sit upon the shoulder of Jesus, he knew this would be the Lamb of God who would take away the sins of the world. John became one of the first to welcome the Savior. Faith is the first essential for all who would be a disciple of Jesus.

Listening to Christ . . . *Contentedly Waiting*

A certain woman named Martha received him into her house. And she had a sister called Mary, which also sat at Jesus' feet, and heard his word (Luke 10:38–39).

Mary of Bethany was a contemplative woman and totally different from her sister. Martha was an industrious lady, very capable of managing her kitchen. Faith and works could be seen together every day in that hospitable home. When the elder sister informed Mary that guests had been invited for dinner, she did not realize that repercussions would disturb the tranquillity of the family. Mary became instantly fascinated by Jesus, and forgetting the necessity of being a hostess, she sat on the floor eagerly awaiting every word spoken. She had already welcomed the Lord into her heart and home. Now she wished to learn, and even the Lord was delighted to have such an attentive listener.

This is the second phase of Christian education. When the Savior enters into a life, He desires to be the center and circumference of it; everything should revolve around Him. A healthy Christian can never hear too much about Christ, whose words are a benediction and never a bore! When a man is too busy to listen to the Master, he resembles a space rocket that is about to crash! History teaches that all outstanding leaders of the church were devoted to the Scriptures. They believed "That man shall not live by bread alone, but by every word of God" (Luke 4:4).

Living for Christ . . . *Consecrated Walking*

He that saith he abideth in him ought himself so to walk, even
as he walked (1 John 2:6).

The apostle John was annoyed. He had been opposed by a
man who was obsessed with his own importance. His associates
claimed to be Christians, but their conduct left much to be desired. When he wrote to Gaius, the apostle said, "I wrote unto
the church: but Diotrophes, who loveth to have the preeminence
among them, receiveth us not. Wherefore, if I come, I will remember his deeds which he doeth, prating against us with mali-
cious words: and not content therewith, neither doth he himself
receive the brethren, and forbiddeth them that would, and casteth
them out of the church" (3 John 9–10). It was inconceivable that
he who had leaned upon the Lord's bosom should be opposed by
a man whose criticisms divided an assembly. Some of the devoted brethren had been compelled to leave the fellowship. John
was very indignant, and his words revealed the intensity of his
feelings. Any person who claims to be a believer should be
Christlike. Pious words are meaningless rhetoric unless they are
spoken by loving people. Evidently Diotrophes was a man obsessed with himself. He did not understand that his conduct was
outrageous.

It was to be expected that after Mary of Bethany had listened
to Jesus, she would do what He suggested. The Lord said that if
people loved God, they would keep His commandments. Men
should be able to watch Christians and come face-to-face with
the Savior.

Leaning on Christ . . . *Conscientiously Worshiping*

Now there was leaning on Jesus' bosom one of his disciples,
whom Jesus loved (John 13:23).

It may be significant that John was the only disciple who
leaned upon the Savior's bosom. It may even be more indicative
that none of the other men desired to emulate his example. Had
there been someone else who wished to do so, he could have
shared John's privilege. It is also extremely interesting to remember that this apostle survived longer than any of his brethren, and his guidance helped the churches to survive fierce

persecution. John was not content to remain a yard away from his Lord, when it was possible to get closer. He was as weary as the others, but when it was possible to rest he leaned upon the bosom of his Lord where it became possible to feel heartbeats and hear quiet whispers. Did the remaining disciples dismiss John's act as sentimental? Were they too blind to recognize that the secret of tranquillity was found only in close proximity to the Savior? John would have appreciated the words of John G. Whittier who wrote:

> Drop Thy still dews of quietness
> Till all our strivings cease;
> Take from our lives the strain and stress,
> And let our ordered lives confess
> The beauty of Thy peace.

Laboring for Christ . . . *Consistently Working*

We then, as workers together with him, beseech you also that ye receive not the grace of God in vain (2 Cor. 6:1).

For we are laborers together with God (1 Cor. 3:9).

Paul rejoiced in the company of young men for whom he was an example and guide. He never asked any of his helpers to do something he was unwilling to do himself. John Mark, Timothy, Silas, and Titus were all student companions of the great missionary, and others mentioned in the Pauline epistles were said to be *"fellow-laborers"* and fellow servants (see Phil. 4:3 and Col. 1:7). The apostle emphasized that "we are laborers together *with* God." It was always a privilege to work *for* the Lord, but it is infinitely better to work *with* Him.

If we may use modern terms, it means the employer is always on the job to counsel, direct, and help His servants. Even the most unlovely place on earth can become radiant when God is present. Mission stations in uncivilized parts of the world may seem like heaven when the presence of the Lord is recognized and enjoyed. Nevertheless, even the most dedicated missionaries may become dejected, lonely, and irritable if they forget that God shares every experience. Martha was very frustrated when she criticized her sister, yet when she began thinking about her

Guest, the tension eased, and the kitchen became paradise. When Jesus commissioned the disciples to evangelize the world, He promised to be with them *always*. No worker for Christ need ever labor alone.

Longing for Christ . . . *Continually Wanting*

For our conversation [citizenship] is in heaven; from whence also we look for the Saviour (Phil. 3:20).

The apostle Paul was convinced the Savior would return to earth and that human bodies would be transformed into His likeness. Pain, sickness, deformity, and age would disappear forever. Throughout history that fact has been the hope and inspiration of the church. At any moment during his illustrious career Paul would have gladly welcomed his Lord. Nevertheless, he was not content to sit idly waiting for that moment. He determined to "work while it was day for the night would come when no man could work." So well did he perform his ministry that, by the end of his lifetime the known world had heard the good news of salvation through Christ. He believed that "here we have no continuing city, but we seek one to come" (see Heb. 13:14). To the Christians in Philippi, he wrote: "For I am in a strait betwixt two, having a desire to depart, and to be with Christ; which is far better: Nevertheless to abide in the flesh is more needful for you" (Phil. 1:23–24). From the moment when he enlisted in God's army until the day he received his reward for meritorious service, Paul never faltered.

These six phases of Christian experience represent the complete life of a Christian warrior. (1) Looking at Christ; (2) Listening to Christ; (3) Living for Christ; (4) Leaning on Christ; (5) Laboring for Christ; (6) Longing for Christ. These are milestones along the Christian highway. Blessed is the man who at the end of the journey can say:

For I am now ready to be offered, and the time of my departure is at hand. I have fought a good fight, I have finished my course, I have kept the faith. Henceforth there is laid up for me a crown of righteousness, which the Lord, the righteous judge, shall give me at that day: and not to me only, but unto all them also that love his appearing (2 Tim. 4:6–8).

> *Unto him that loved us, and washed us from our sins in his*
> *own blood, and hath made us kings and priests unto God and*
> *his Father; to him be glory and dominion for ever and ever.*
> *Amen (Rev. 1:5–6).*

A native Chinese woman who had become a Christian sought membership in the local church. As was the custom, she was required to give her testimony before the leaders of the mission. The chairman asked, "Do you believe that Jesus had sin?" She answered immediately, "Yes, He had sin." Thinking the candidate had misunderstood the question, the missionary rephrased it but received the same answer. He then asked, "Do you think I have sin?" She was a little embarrassed, but after a moment's hesitation replied, "You have no sin." Nonplussed the man asked, "How can you believe Jesus the Son of the great God had sin, and yet you believe I am without sin?" She answered, "I believe Jesus had sin because *He took mine.*"

At the close of an evangelistic service, a very argumentative woman was furious because she disagreed with my message. She said I was a deceiver of the people and then claimed she was not a sinner. I said, "Lady, are you telling me that from January to December you never made a mistake. You never sinned—not even once?" She replied, "That is correct, and when you say all people are sinners you mislead your listeners." I asked her scared husband if he agreed with his wife's statement, but the poor fellow was too frightened to be honest. I informed her that according to the Scriptures she was untruthful, for John said, "If we say that we have no sin, we deceive ourselves, and the truth is not in us" (1 John 1:8). She was very angry and shouted, "He was as wrong as you are." Her raucous voice was causing a disturbance, so I said, "Lady, will you do something for me?" She answered, "What?" "Please go away and do not return." There was a great difference between the woman in China and the one who disliked me, but I am convinced all intelligent people would know which was the wiser woman.

Our Sins . . . *Condemning*

For our transgressions are multiplied before thee, and *our sins* testify against us: for our transgressions are with us; and as for our iniquities, we know them (Isa. 59:12).

Isaiah was a prophet who recognized reality. He knew God and was aware of his own shortcomings. That he was morally and spiritually better than his contemporaries was unimportant. He had sinned against God and his own conscience. The best way to prove a cane is warped is to place it alongside one that is straight. The most convincing proof that a man is a sinner is to compare him with the Savior. A person who cannot see is blind. Anyone unable to see fault in himself is in darkness.

The apostle John, describing the Day of Judgment, said: "And I saw the dead, small and great, stand before God; and the books were opened: and another book was opened, which is the book of life: and the dead were judged out of those things which were written in the books, according to their works. And the sea gave up the dead which were in it; and death and hell delivered up the dead which were in them: and they were judged every man according to their works" (Rev. 20:12–13). Unforgiven sin causes grief in this world and eternal sorrow in that which is yet to be.

Our Sins . . . *Considered*

For I delivered unto you first of all that which I also received, how that Christ died for *our sins* according to the scriptures (1 Cor. 15:3).

When Peter addressed the crowd at the Feast of Pentecost, he made a remarkable statement. "But those things, which God before had shewed by the mouth of all his prophets, that Christ should suffer, he hath so fulfilled" (Acts 3:18). God knew what would happen when He sent His Son to earth. The crucifixion of the Savior did not surprise the Almighty. He knew from eternal ages His Son would be nailed to a cross. That He revealed this fact through *all* the prophets proved this thought was on His mind throughout Old Testament generations. God was continually aware of human need. The apostle John described the Lord as being "the Lamb slain from *the foundation of the world*" (Rev. 13:8).

The gulf between the holiness of God and the sinfulness of men seemed impossible to span, but the Lord found a way to

210

bridge it and make access to God possible. It is commonly believed that dialogue is better than armed aggression. When men discuss their grievances, problems are often removed. Heaven provided the first example of that important fact. The difficulty of securing redemption for undeserving sinners appeared to be insurmountable, but when the members of the Divine Family discussed the matter, they solved the problem.

Our Sins . . . *Compelling*

> And ye know that he was manifested to take away *our sins*; and in him is no sin (1 John 3:5).

Christ came into this world to manifest, to reveal, to make known, to explain the perfect will of God. Primarily, He did not come to perform all kinds of physical miracles, nor even to introduce higher and better laws. He came to take away our sins. The Lord had considered the consequences of human guilt but finally was compelled to act. Since all humans were sinners, and even the angelic world had been tainted by the fall of Lucifer, there was no one available to handle the problem of sin. Even if there had been some special person able to commence the task, he would have been unable to complete the work. Paul wrote: "For whom he did foreknow, he also did predestinate *to be conformed to the image of his Son*" (Rom. 8:29). If the Savior had remained indifferent to human need, His tranquillity would have been ruined by memories. John wrote: "But whoso hath this world's good, and seeth his brother have need, and shutteth up his bowels of compassion from him, how dwelleth the love of God in him?" (1 John 3:17). He who had been the Lamb slain from the foundation of the world (Rev. 13:8), and who had by type and prediction indicated what was to happen came to complete what had been commenced. God's magnificent plan was fulfilled at Calvary when the Savior's cry echoed around the world—"*Tetelestai—It is finished.*"

Our Sins . . . *Canceled*

"And he is the propitiation for *our sins*: and not for ours only, but also for the sins of the whole world" (1 John 2:2).

The Greek word used here is *ilasmos*. It is one of three used in the New Testament to teach the doctrine of the Atonement.

The other two are *estallagee* and *apolurposi*. *The Pulpit Commentary* states the collective interpretation suggests the idea of the "redemption of the offending party *by payment of the debt.*" Paul also said, "Being justified freely by his grace through the redemption that is in Christ Jesus: Whom God hath set forth to be a propitiation through faith in his blood, to declare his righteousness for the remission of sins that are past, through the forbearance of God" (Rom. 3:24–25).

A debt that has been canceled signifies the debtor is free from responsibility. His indebtedness no longer exists. The word propitiation that occurs three times in the New Testament (Rom. 3:25; 1 John 2:2; 1 John 4:10) expresses the idea of an offender being restored to favor. He who was far from God has been brought near by the blood of Jesus (see Eph. 2:13). These Scriptures reveal the situation as it is seen by God; our record before the Almighty is without blemish. We are justified—*"just if we'd* never sinned."

Our Sins . . . *Cleansed*

Who being the brightness of his glory, and the express image of his person, and upholding all things by the word of his power, when he had by himself purged *our sins*, sat down on the right hand of the Majesty on high (Heb. 1:3).

Without assistance from anyone, Christ did what had to be done. He purged—*He washed away our sins.* The earlier texts revealed how God sees us *in heaven.* This verse explains how He sees us *on earth.* We are *in Christ* and cleansed from sin. When the Lord spoke to Jeremiah, He said, "I will forgive their iniquity, and I will remember their sin no more" (Jer. 31:34). John, writing to his converts, said: "I write unto you, little children, because your sins *are forgiven* you for his name's sake" (1 John 2:12). He did not promise this would be a reward when people stand before God. Forgiveness can be received and enjoyed *now.*

I knew a very sincere and talented lady who was never able to accept this gracious fact. Apparently when she was a child, she did something that she regretted throughout her life. When that woman heard my wife speaking about forgiveness, she exclaimed, "Oh, no, no, no, I cannot be forgiven for what I did to my sister." She was unable to forgive herself and therefore could not

212

believe her heavenly Father could forgive and forget her child-hood behavior. There will be no sin in heaven, and if one blem-ish remained, entrance would be denied. Happy and safe is the person who can say:

> Gone, gone, gone, gone,
> Yes, my sins are gone.
> Now my soul is free,
> And in my heart's a song.
> Buried in the deepest sea;
> Yes, that's good enough for me.
> I shall live eternally,
> Praise God, my sins are gone.

Our Sins . . . *Conquered*

Unto him that loved us, and washed (loosed us, RV) us from *our sins* in his own blood (Rev. 1:5).

The Greek word translated *washed* is *lousanti*, and most of the translations render it *loosed* or *freed from*. It has often been said that Christ saves from the penalty, power, and presence of sin. The first was accomplished when the Lord took our sins upon Himself. The second is being perfected now by the Holy Spirit who resides within God's people. The third will be com-pleted when the Lord takes His people to be with Himself. All of these are phases in God's redemptive plan for mankind. Never-theless, believers continue to struggle with spiritual problems. Even Paul said, "For I know that in me (that is, in my flesh), dwelleth no good thing: for to will is present with me; but how to perform that which is good I find not. For the good that I would I do not: but the evil which I would not, that I do" (Rom. 7:18–19).

Christians resemble Simon Peter whose exuberant faith en-abled him to walk upon the water and who began to sink the moment he ceased looking at his Lord. He might have drowned had not the Savior reached down to rescue His friend. Many depressed believers seem to spend more time sinking than look-ing! Nevertheless, Christ has the ability to impart the strength which alone enables people to walk on their own stormy seas!

Our Sins . . . *Challenged*

Our Lord Jesus Christ, Who gave himself for *our sins*, that he might deliver us from this present evil world, according to the will of God and our Father (Gal. 1:3–4).

The Lord Jesus Christ: Who shall change our vile body, that it may be fashioned like unto his glorious body, according to the working whereby he is able even to subdue all things unto himself (Phil. 3:20–21).

What Christ accomplished at the cross assures us that even the last stain of sin will be removed, its power destroyed, and its effect upon redeemed souls terminated. Sin prevented Adam and Eve from remaining in the Garden of Eden. It would likewise prevent entry into God's eternal kingdom, for "nothing that defileth shall enter therein." When God's children are taken to the place of many mansions, sin will never again cause problems. Even their bodies will be miraculously changed. Alas, even Christians are conscious of evil within their souls. Satan has a workshop within every believer, but this will be destroyed forever. "We shall be like Him, for we shall see Him as he is." The last challenge of evil will have been overcome, and heaven will not have a single blemish.

The seven texts used in this study have certain things in common. They emphasize the fact of sin and state the only remedy for the ills of men and women is Christ and His precious blood. It is significant that the authors of the New Testament were not content to write about Jesus of Nazareth. His glorious deeds and triumphant living could only supply an example for human beings, and since men and women do not possess the ability to live as He did, the end result could only have been condemnation. When the apostles referred to the blood of Christ, they were explaining this represented the sinless life of the Lord outpoured at Calvary. The early Christians were convinced that without the death of Christ there could be no eternal life for sinners. Happy are those people who understand the cross is the gateway to the stars!

*And the Spirit and the bride say, Come. And let him that heareth
say, Come. And let him that is athirst, come. And whosoever will,
let him take the water of life freely (Rev. 22:17).*

The river Jordan was always a lifeline for the people of Palestine. Throughout the long history of the Hebrew people water was a priceless commodity. Long ago herdsmen fought for the possession of wells, and during recent hostilities when Syria planned to divert its waters, the Israeli Air Force promptly bombed the factories where the necessary machinery was being prepared. The nation could not exist without water, which is mainly derived from rainfall and resultant wells, springs, and underground supplies. The city of Jericho is supplied by the spring of Elisha, but in other areas drought is a constant menace. The modern state of Israel has performed miracles in transforming deserts into gardens, but even its ingenuity has been challenged by the ever-increasing need for moisture. Today drinking water is being made by desalination plants, but in other parts of the country this is not possible. The production of many kinds of fruit depends upon irrigation and is one of the nation's most important exports.

It was to be expected that ancient prophets would take advantage of the national need and in their writings use the country's water as an illustration of spiritual truth. Furthermore, the fact that water came from rain suggested that only Jehovah could supply what Israel needed. David had military might and wealth. Solomon, for a time at least, had wisdom, but without water the royal household would have perished. When the prayer of Elijah closed the heavens for a period of three and a half years, the entire nation faced insurmountable obstacles. It was only the reappearance of Elijah that saved the people from disaster. The apostle John was aware of the situation, and it is extremely interesting to discover that he repeatedly referred to man's need for *living water.*

Salvation Offered . . . *How Simple*
And whosoever will, let him take the water of life freely
(Rev. 22:17).

When John wrote the book of Revelation, he was careful to quote the words of the Savior. "I Jesus have sent mine angel to testify unto you these things in the churches" (Rev. 22:16). The messengers of heaven were instructed to urge all nations to come to Christ for spiritual refreshment. Yet each person was requested *to take* the water of life freely. There was no need to seek supplies. They had already been provided. There were no restrictions. Every person from every land was welcome to share in the provision. Whosoever included everybody. Yet certain things were evident. First, people had to *recognize* their need—they were thirsty. Secondly, they were required to respond and *come*. Thirdly, they had to *take* what was being offered.

The Savior emphasized similar truths when He spoke about the marriage of the king's son. He described a man who was found without a wedding garment. Monarchs prepared such apparel so that the celebrations would be exceptionally beautiful. The guests who had been brought from the streets could not be embarrassed, for their ragged clothing was hidden beneath the king's garment. Unfortunately, one man was conspicuous among the guests, for his appearance contrasted with that of the other people. Since the gifts were offered at the door, it was evident this man was satisfied with what he had. He was expelled from the banquet and lived to regret his folly (see Matt. 22:8–14).

Water can be expensive in drought-ravaged countries. It is never free. During one of my visits to Egypt I flew from Cairo to Luxor, and as the plane followed the course of the Nile, adjacent areas seemed to be as a green canal going through a desert. The Egyptian government, with the aid of foreign investments, built the Aswan Dam so that water could be stored and later released to irrigate the lowlands. Yet even the impoverished farmers, in one way or another, are required to pay for this service. When the Savior announced that people could take of the water of life *freely*, He was endorsing what Paul said to the Christians in Rome. "He that spared not his own Son, but delivered him up for us all, how shall he not with him also *freely give us all things*" (Rom. 8:32).

Satisfaction Overwhelming . . . *How Sufficient*

Jesus answered and said unto her, Whosoever drinketh of this water shall thirst again: But whosoever shall drink of the water that I shall give him shall never thirst; but the water that I shall give him shall be in him a well of water springing up into everlasting life (John 4:13–14).

The woman who met the Lord at Sychar's well was fascinated, surprised, and confused. To meet anyone at midday was completely unexpected, for at that hour citizens were preparing for their siesta. That a Jew should ask a Samaritan for anything was, to say the least, amazing. Ordinary men would prefer to remain thirsty than to fraternize with despised outsiders. This Man was an enigma; He spoke of drawing water from a well when He had no container nor rope necessary to complete the task. He spoke of religion as though He was a qualified rabbi who disdained the criticism of other Jews. The Stranger was aware of the temples on Mount Gerazim and in Jerusalem, and yet in some mysterious manner He seemed unconcerned. He said that God should be worshiped in spirit and truth and suggested that human temples superseded all others. This man was surely a prophet, for He knew the secrets of her life. His claim to be able to supply living water was intriguing. It has often been said this woman came with her water pot to draw water from the well, but after speaking with Christ, she ran away with the well!

The conversation bequeathed to later generations spiritual treasure. It is refreshing to discover water in a wilderness, but even more wonderful to discover an *active spring* which is a guarantee of a continuing supply. The Savior did not differentiate between the well and the spring, for they belonged to each other. If the one ceased to exist, the well would become empty, and people would only be helped for a limited time. The provision of God never runs dry, but rubbish can hinder the flow of water.

It is probably one of the greatest tragedies within the modern church that revival has ceased to exist. The rubbish of this world has choked and filled the well. Isaac recognized a similar fact when he ordered his servants to reopen the well which had been dug by his father, Abraham (see Gen. 26:18–19). Christians need continuing supplies of spiritual refreshment. Men dying of thirst can hardly find comfort in memories of water enjoyed many years earlier. God desires His children to be filled with the Holy Spirit. It is a glorious experience to discover living water, but unless the spring *fills* the soul, the purposes of the Savior are thwarted. God gives what is necessary, but men are required to draw from His wells. The prophet Isaiah said, "Therefore with joy shall ye draw water out of the wells of salvation" (Isa. 12:3).

Service Outreaching . . . *How Splendid*

In the last day, that great day of the feast Jesus stood and cried, saying, If any man thirst, let him come unto me, and drink. He that believeth on me, as the scripture hath said, out of his belly shall flow rivers of living water. (But this spake he of the Spirit, which they that believe on him should receive: for the Holy Ghost was not yet given; because that Jesus was not yet glorified) (John 7:37–39).

It is not necessary to pump water from a well when springs are continually active. To be filled with the Holy Spirit is the natural sequence of being regenerated. There is never need to persuade dedicated Christians to serve the Savior. Automatically, instinctively, living energy flows from their souls to enrich impoverished people.

The tragedy within the modern church is that Christians do not enjoy the benefit of a full and overflowing soul. True Christians radiate benedictions even when they are unaware of the fact.

The great evangelist D. L. Moody often explained how his life was revolutionized. He said he had done his best to extend the kingdom of Christ but knew something was lacking in his ministry. Then came the experience when his entire being was flooded with a new sense of the Divine Presence. He preached old sermons, and miracles began to happen. He said, "One day in New York; what a day! I cannot describe it; I seldom talk about it. It is almost too sacred to name. I can only say that God revealed Himself to me. I had such an experience of love that I had to ask Him to stay His hand. I went to preaching again. The sermons were no different. I did not present any new truth. Yet hundreds were converted. I would not be back where I was before that blessed experience."

The outpouring of the power of the Holy Spirit was made possible by the coronation of the Lord, and that fact has remained unchanged. It is only when the Savior becomes the supreme Lord of the Christian's life that God can open the floodgates of heaven to release the power that turns ordinary people into mighty servants of the Most High. Education is of immense value to a minister, but even academic honors cannot be an effective substitute for the anointing of the Holy Spirit. The Savior was correct when He said, "But ye shall receive power, after that the Holy Ghost is come upon you: and ye shall be witnesses unto me both in Jerusalem, and in all Judaea, and in Samaria, and unto the uttermost part of the earth" (Acts 1:8). The followers of Christ should be aware of three facts. (1) Unless a man is born of the Spirit, he remains dead. (2) If a man is not filled with the Spirit, he will always be defeated. (3) If living water does not flow from a man's soul, he will always be disappointing and useless in extending the kingdom of Christ.

SCRIPTURE TEXT INDEX

223

Books by Ivor Powell

Bible Cameos
Vivid biographies of eighty Bible characters—full of helpful hints for sermon preparation.

ISBN 0-8254-3515-3   **192 pp.**   **paperback**

Bible Names of Christ
The author, in his gifted manner, presents eighty short studies on the names and titles of Christ.

ISBN 0-8254-3530-7   **176 pp.**   **paperback**

Bible Nuggets
These thirty-four insightful studies of Bible characters provide enjoyable and challenging reading for pastors and teachers alike.

ISBN 0-8254-3512-9   **192 pp.**   **paperback**

Bible Oases
The author provides the pastor, Bible student, and Christian reader with a look at "less popular portions" of the Bible and their significance for our lives.

ISBN 0-8254-3520-x   **192 pp.**   **paperback**

Bible Promises
A look at the promises of the Bible and their significance to the believer.

ISBN 0-8254-3542-0   **192 pp.**   **paperback**

Bible Windows
A rich collection of over eighty carefully chosen illustrations to better communicate the gospel message and bring to life the key points of its message.

ISBN 0-8254-3522-6   **180 pp.**   **paperback**

Heaven: My Father's Country
What is heaven like? You might be surprised! Ivor Powell examines both the Old and New Testaments to gather a biblical description of "the Father's country."

ISBN 0-8254-3517-x   **144 pp.**   **paperback**